The Divine Heart of Darkness

Finding God in the Shadows

— CATHERINE BIRD —

Sacristy Press
PO Box 612, Durham, DH1 9HT

www.sacristy.co.uk

First published in 2017 by Sacristy Press, Durham

Sacristy Limited, registered in England & Wales, number 7565667

British Library Cataloguing-in-Publication Data
A catalogue record for the book is available from the British Library

ISBN 978-1-910519-58-5

For the community of Svalbard Kirke

Foreword

I regard the words and wisdom in this book as coming from a true guru. There are many ways to define a guru, as leader, guide, or teacher, for example. Central to the concept of guru is wisdom. A true guru speaks and acts from a deep pool and school of wisdom. This is also the primary biblical insight. God, our great and true Guru, is present in and speaks and acts and creates everything out of the primordial deep and darkness (Genesis 1:1–2). Everything flows from this in the Bible. In my view the two opening verses of the Bible summarize its whole content. All that follows these two opening verses illustrates the creative and life-giving God who is with people and accompanies them in all experiences. All life is dark and deep, chaotic and formless. God is always present in it, creating, speaking wisdom, and making all things new (Isaiah 43:19; 65:17; Revelation 21:5).

"The earth was a formless void and darkness covered the face of the deep, while the spirit of God swept over the face of the waters" (Genesis 1:2). God is said to dwell in "formless void and darkness", and from here to do the work of creation. This is God the great and true Guru. Present in the dark and the deep. Creating in the dark and the deep. Recalling that this God is described elsewhere in the Bible as an eagle watching its nest, hovering over its young (Deuteronomy 32:11). And the darkness and the deep is described as a trembling, a disturbance, a stirring, or a storm (Jeremiah 23:9; Daniel 7:2; John 5:7). In Sanskrit the word is "vritti", which signifies a whirlpool. This is what precedes and accompanies creation in Genesis 1. It does not speak of creation out of nothing (ex nihilo). God dwells in and creates within and out of all that is represented by the darkness and the deep.

God calls on all people then to provide care for all created things, and to do all things with wisdom (Genesis 1:26–28). The work of any true guru is to model exactly that. To be prepared to dwell in darkness, to accompany people in darkness, and to do all things with wisdom. A true guru will not lead people from darkness to light. A true guru will sit in the darkness with people and help them to find wisdom from the deep, and stillness within the stirring of life and the whirlpool of the mind. A true guru does not say there is a silver lining to every cloud, and does not speak of light at the end of the tunnel. A true guru is tuned in to the attendance and echo of God in the storm, points to God in the shadows, and helps people to see darkness as a place of sacredness, not scaredness. So a true guru will not hurry people out of darkness, or speak negatively of emptiness, but revel in its holiness.

Cathy does not belittle the fact that many associate despair and difficulties with darkness. She writes, for example, about the experiences of people enslaved in dungeons, without any kind of light, and of refugees in camps without light.

Like a true guru Cathy describes herself as a "friend of darkness", and is not seeking to dispel darkness but sees herself as "turning the dark on" and making it "visible", and wants her readers to experience the "caress of the twilight". She does not want darkness to be eliminated by light but wants "darkness made visible by the light", and wants to draw us to "darkness which gives life to light itself". Cathy reminds us that we need the dark to help us see the light. She insists that darkness is a holding place rather than a hiding place and that "all clear understanding is grounded in the darkness of God". Darkness is a place and time of sacredness, not scaredness. Cathy takes her readers on a journey into darkness portrayed in art, music, hymns, poetry, games, and animals and fish that flourish in the dark and at night. She wants hymn writers to find hope and wisdom in darkness.

Cathy's reflections on death as entering darkness are so helpful. She writes of "the ultimate paradox of the Christian faith that love leads to grief" and of "darkness as a metaphor for what is surely the ultimate transfer of trust ... from life to death", and reflects well on this. In her words, "we think that light is the source of life – yet it is in darkness that all living things have their naissance, in the womb, in the earth, in the seed, in the tomb, the absence of light is necessary for life to take hold." Entrance into darkness is not an entrance into disintegration and disappearance, it is an entrance into a place of recreation into new life.

I am grateful to Cathy for her Dark Creed celebrating God as creator and prince of darkness, and as inner shadow. Some readers may struggle with this, but it is offered here as a way of opening up new ways to reflect on God, without wanting to limit or restrict God. The Dark Creed, and indeed all that Cathy shares in this book, challenges us all to examine how we use and understand and speak of light and darkness. What do you normally associate with darkness and light? How do you use the concepts of darkness and light in your prayers and worship and liturgy? Darkness is abundant and life-giving, as light is. Darkness and light are friends, and both are gifts of God. Cathy provides profound theological reflections on darkness. She takes us into explorations of darkness and calls us not to be afraid.

Many years ago I bought a copy of the book *The Owl Who Was Afraid of the Dark* by Jill Tomlinson (Methuen & Co Ltd, 1968) to help children overcome fear of dark. I would buy and give Cathy's book to adults who are afraid of the dark. And also to those who enjoy or see sacredness in darkness. It is a pleasurable read and reclaims darkness. It makes it possible to see God as darkness as well as light. Cathy Bird amplifies the positive message of darkness, and she has done it with meticulous research, challenge, and wisdom.

On camping holidays I take great delight in sitting outside the tent to watch the sunset, being embraced by the twilight, and seeing the darkness as it visibly comes on and deepens. Everyone heads indoors, and even the birds return home. And on a clear night I see the stars slowly become visible, and quite bright, and sometimes a fleeting shooting star too. Often I lie down on the ground and find myself in the sky. Just me and the stars with their myriad patterns and pathways. The star-studded Milky Way beats any red carpet laid out for celebrities. I merge with the stars. This is the revelation and gift of darkness; light hides and covers it. I find it so hard to leave the aura and awe-inspiring company of these jewels of the sky. It is a sadness to part from this company. It is I who turns away, not the stars.

Reading this book is like sitting in the dark with a trusted friend who shares your delight in darkness and points out the different stars, and is a shooting star or comet herself or himself in a sky full of stars.

Inderjit Bhogal
June 2017

Acknowledgements

There are many people to thank, and many reasons to be thankful.

I must start by giving credit to all those who have influenced my thinking, and whose writing, ideas, suggestions and comments have, in one way or another, found their way onto these pages.

Then I must send love to all my family, friends and colleagues who have lived with this idea for some years now, and who have all, in many different ways, helped a germ of an idea to flourish. For their specific but varied contributions I want to name Meg Bird, Peter Bird, Barbara Cooper, Pauline Barnett, Eve Watmore, Hazel Forecast, Ron Smith, Jenny Smith, John Cooke, Robert Beckford, Joanne Cox-Darling, Bonni Belle Pickard, David Hardman, Simon Cooper, Jenny Cooper, Ann Bird, Derek Bird, Andrew Bird, Jacqui Bird, Michaela Youngson, Tamsin Youngson, Roderick Leece, Sarika Bose, Tirthankar Bose, Mandakranta Bose, Jørgen Skov Sørensen, Deborah Powers, Peter Powers, Roger Watkins, and Margaret Glover.

For words of encouragement at just the right time, I am grateful to the following people: the late Geoff Cornell (for telling me to get on with it! I am sorry you will not get to read the final result, you are missed), Peter Clark, for getting what I was talking about at a very early stage and sending me a movie, and Roger Sawtell, for reminding me how many rejections J. K. Rowling received before Harry Potter was finally published!

In particular I want to express deep gratitude to those who read the manuscript at various points in its formation: Inderjit Bhogal, for telling me to stop reading other people's books and to just get on and write my own; Graeme Watson, for honest and constructive feedback; Sara Maitland, for telling me my writing was sane when many others were implying otherwise; and Censis Berzins, the Comma King.

I have only recently come to know the artist Bjørn Strandenes, whose sublime artwork adorns this book. I am privileged to have received his gift and I leave you, the reader, to discern whether or not this particular book should be judged by its cover!

Without the inspiration offered by the context of the Arctic Polar Night I doubt I would have ever started writing. So above all, I am grateful to the community of Svalbard Kirke for the gracious friendship and hospitality that made my visits possible. In particular to Leif Magne Helgesen, Torunn Sørenson, Anne Lise Klungseth Sandvik, Regina Lorig, Kim Holmén and Janet Holmén. Longyearbyen is forever in my heart. I'll be back soon. Just not in the summer!

Cathy Bird
September 2017

It is pitch dark . . . when the Moths arrive . . . the darkness is so profound that even in the open air . . . it is hardly possible to see one's hand before one's face.

Clusters of bushy shrubs make a rampart . . . It is through this tangle of branches, in complete darkness, that the Great Peacock has to tack about to reach the object of his pilgrimage. The Moth . . . goes forward without hesitating and passes through without knocking against things. He directs his tortuous flight so skilfully that, despite the obstacles overcome, he arrives . . . with not a scratch upon him. The darkness is light enough for him.

J. H. Fabre, **The Life of the Caterpillar,** *1916*

Contents

Introduction

I

I want to introduce to you my friend, the darkness. Truth be told, darkness is more than a friend to me. Darkness is a companion, a co-conspirator, a muse. When darkness goes away I long for darkness to return. When darkness is maligned and slandered, I want to defend darkness. You may say it sounds as if I am in love with darkness, and it would be hard for me to deny it.

My purpose in writing this book is to spread that love. Drawing together evidence, experience, and research from a wide variety of traditions—historical, scientific, liturgical, artistic, and religious—combined with the personal, anecdotal, experiential, and the shamelessly nostalgic, I hope to be able to open up a new dialogue. I want to ask how we can move closer towards a positive experience of darkness such that it can lift our spirits, challenge our hearts and minds, and draw us closer into the heart of God. This is a book for people who want to ask questions about God, and who want to be challenged about what they believe, say, and do. It offers a place for questioning the things that many think to be unquestionable—not to deny God, but to find a fuller understanding of how God works within human experience. I hope that in reading this book you will be able to lay to one side any of your own preconceptions about darkness. If you are someone who fears the dark, I hope that what you read may help you to be less fearful. Maybe after reading it you will feel brave enough to take a walk outside after sundown and see the evening in a different glow. If the onset of winter has always filled you with dread, and after reading this you are able to put your clock back at the appointed hour and not feel your heart sink quite so much, then it will have served a valuable purpose. If you have hitherto understood and described that which is of God as being light and that which is not of God as darkness, then perhaps what is written here can open up to you a different language, which in turn can reveal a new dimension of the Divine. If, on the other hand, you have always secretly loved the dark but have not been able to name it (for it is still a taboo), then I hope what you read will allow you to emerge from the blinding light and encourage others to see the joy and warmth contained within the shadows.

II

In most forms of the English language darkness is a byword for terrible things, a metaphor for all manner of misery, grief, trauma, illness, or sorrow. At the same time, its more glamorous sibling, light, is used to describe that which is glorious, peaceful, hopeful—the proverbial "light at the end of the (dark) tunnel." In the catalogue of established religious allegory, light and dark are normally juxtaposed as representations of goodness and evil whereby God is the "light" (metaphorically speaking, the healing or the peace) which needs to be experienced in moments and places of "darkness" (sadness, fear, or times of perceived spiritual warfare). Whilst such descriptions usually present darkness as a place of hope, in the sense that it is often in our moments of deepest need that we experience the presence of God most fully, the symbolic connections are essentially such that darkness is the negative state over and within which the light of God needs to shine. That God does indeed meet us in our moments of personal and communal despair is an authentic Christian experience, yet I have gradually become aware of a deep-seated personal unease with the conventional light and darkness metaphor as a means of describing it. Ever since I can remember, and for whatever reason I do not know, I have associated darkness, not with fear and malevolence, but with cosiness, rest, Christmas, an essential element of what the Danes have for years known as "*hygge*" or "the art of creating intimacy".

Alongside that, a growing awareness of the power of language to influence and direct thought and behaviour has led me to ask whether there is a different way of looking at things here, a different perspective, a different point of view that has merit and, perhaps, purpose. For centuries, Christian imperialism has been underpinned by the opposition of Light and Dark and their particular metaphorical nuances. The model of mission which has at its heart the assertion that a metaphorical light is needed (faith in Jesus Christ as Lord and Saviour) to destroy a metaphorical darkness (the absence of such faith) has been responsible for untold atrocities. It is a model which continues to this day to be manifested in forms of Christianity which pursue agendas of homophobia and Islamophobia, for example.

Yet the call to take the "Light" into the "Darkness" is a model of mission which I would argue misrepresents the whole essence of the gospel—a gospel which I prefer to see as being about *revealing* the presence and activity of God, which is *already* present in all things and in all places. It is about drawing people into relationship with that presence and activity, and hence into relationship with one another. If, as I believe, God is as much revealed in darkness as in light, then the metaphorical foundation of a pernicious model of mission falls away. Perhaps, then, just perhaps, a sensible and considered questioning of the very model itself becomes possible, allowing us to move beyond the perceived dualism of all things to embrace a diversity and balance which better reflect Scripture.

Writing this book, and the Dark Creed in particular (see Chapter 8), is, for me, part of a deeper yearning for a Christianity which has at its heart the life and inclusive love of Christ. This is not a Christianity which concerns itself with upholding formulaic doctrine or holds that orthodoxy (belief in the "right" thing) is paramount. It is not a Christianity in which the observance of a particular moral code (the avoidance of sin) or the use of a particular form of language equates with salvation. Rather, this is a Christianity which holds the fragility of the human condition at its centre, a Christianity which envisions the reign of God as the moment in time when all the glorious and magnificent forms of God's creation find fulfilment, acceptance, and connection. So there is a wider agenda here which is about the re-examination of all our ideas about what is beautiful and sacred.

A few modern spiritual writers have dared to challenge the status quo and emphasize the positive nature of darkness. In her book *Findings*, the Scottish poet and nature writer Kathleen Jamie describes her quest to "enter into the dark for the love of its textures and wild intimacy". "Pity the dark:" she says, "we're so concerned to overcome and banish it, it's crammed full of all that's devilish, like some grim cupboard under the stair. But dark is good."[1]

The theologian John Hull, who died suddenly while this book was in formation, wrote from his personal experience of blindness about how he discovered God in darkness. Through a radical re-interpretation of Scripture, he was able to move away from the traditional understanding of God as one who is found only within light and who cherishes light above darkness, to recognize God as one who blesses the darkness, who draws it into the created order, and offers a new identity to those whose blindness excludes them from the world of natural light. He wrote:

> . . . darkness has made progress. At first, it was regarded as a horrifying abyss, an amorphous nothingness, but then it was named and placed within the day. As such it was seen by God to be good. Goodness, however, was not enough. When we reach the seventh day, the darkness is not only good, it is sanctified by God's rest. It is declared to be holy. The darkness is blessed along with the morning and becomes the Sabbath of God. The God who brooded over the darkness, bringing it into the shape of separation and recognizing it, now completes this work by bringing the darkness and the light into a sacred unity.[2]

Most recently, the popular American writer Barbara Brown Taylor, an ordained Episcopalian priest and academic, has offered a significant contribution to the development of thinking in this area. Her book, *Learning to Walk in the Dark*, offers an insightful personal reflection into her own journey towards appreciating the delights of darkness.[3] There are a few others writing in the field of theology, but also in other disciplines, and I am grateful to them all for mentioning the unmentionable and for affirming my own instinct that in darkness is to be found beauty, life, and worth. Chapters 2 and 3 of this work offer an overview of how the Bible and some ancient mystical strands of the Christian tradition have, in the past, offered entirely positive representations of darkness as a state of being and as an allegory for the nature and activity of God. Although these have, over time, become suppressed by the pervasive negative imagery, I attempt to draw attention to them, so opening the way for a different perspective to come to the fore. However, it has to be said that the bulk of literature, both fiction and non-fiction, remains highly deleterious to the reputation of darkness. Darkness and evil have, it seems, become virtually synonymous, and it is the dogmatic nature of this association that I am seeking to nudge here. If, as Psalm 139 says, both light and dark are equal in the experience of the Divine, why is it that light has come to be exalted, venerated, worshipped even, whilst darkness has become demonized and feared?

Has the common and apparently unquestioning acceptance that darkness is bad and light is good led to a particular way of thinking, not only about God, but also about human nature and the natural world, perhaps even about darkness itself? A particular way of thinking which distances God from human suffering, renders the human condition irrevocably fearful of the dark, and leaves darkness, shade, and shadow as things to be avoided at all costs.

III

As I contemplated the writing of this book, I used the gift of a sabbatical from my day job as a Methodist minister to travel to a true place of darkness. In search of the darkest place on earth, the World Wide Web directed me to Svalbard, a Norwegian archipelago lying some 400 miles north of the mainland and deep within the Arctic Circle. Between October and February, Svalbard experiences a "Polar Night" when the sun does not show its face above the horizon, and the landscape is plunged into a constant state of lightlessness. Day is as dark as night and night is as dark as day. I wondered whether people for whom the concentrated periods of darkness are part of a regular pattern of life would recognize and own the "evil darkness" metaphor, and how an absence of light affects the soul and the psyche. Svalbard is home to the most northerly inhabited places on earth. In fact, it is home to several "most northerly" titles. The world's most northerly jacuzzi, the world's most northerly bar, and the world's most northerly church! It was within the warmth of the community of that church, Svalbard Kirke in Longyearbyen, that I began in earnest my attempt to defend the darkness. This book is not a travel journal, but the experience of living in constant darkness for sixteen days had a profound impact. So much so that I have since returned to Svalbard twice: once, at the end of the Polar Night season, to share in the celebrations of the community as the sun rises for the first time over the horizon; then, at a very different time of year, when the long light days of the Midnight Sun come to an end and the people prepare for the return of the dark season. These visits have been both a challenge to, and ultimately a confirmation of, my passion for darkness. The conversations and encounters I have had with those for whom the extremes of light and dark are a part of the normal cycle of life have informed my thinking and opened my mind. Consequently, at various points in the book I offer some reflections from Svalbard—either my own or those with whom I have lived and talked—which lie in the shade of the main text.

IV

At various points in the book I make mention of paintings which it has not been possible to reproduce here, and some songs and pieces of music. Where possible I invite you, as you read, to search online and find the item in question, so as to be able to appreciate more fully the points I am trying to make. Because a strong motivation for my writing is to encourage a reconsideration of the traditional Christian language and symbolism relating to darkness, I have also included some original liturgical material which attempts to demonstrate how this might be done. Some of it might seem shocking—Jesus as the "Prince of Darkness", for example—but I ask you to hold it gently while you read. It is offered from a place of genuine struggle and delicate faith. I hope that, in time, my attempts will continue to open up ways of thinking about that fundamental state from which all creation sprang. Whilst I may appear at times to fall into the same trap as some of the traditions and writers of whom I am critical for their unquestioning demonization of the darkness (by, in my own way, demonizing the light), it is not my intention to throw the proverbial light baby out with the dark and dingy bathwater! It is simply my hope that in what follows I am able to retrieve the reputation of darkness in the pursuit of a "spirituality of balance",[4] so that it may take its rightful place alongside light as a state of being which is necessary for life, fruitful in character, and utterly divine.

Svalbard Journey
First Visit, 6 January 2013

Any journey knowingly undertaken on the feast day of Epiphany is likely to be tinged with mystery and expectation. I set off in pursuit of the darkness, following—like the Magi, those strangely enigmatic, yet oh-so-familiar astrologers—a fragile premise, an idea, a hope; not exactly certain where I am heading or what to expect but in anticipation of discovery and learning, holding fast to the potential and possibility of my wild imagining.

As the plane takes off from Oslo in the last vestiges of the southern Norwegian daylight, I am conscious of the fact that this will be the last I will see of the sun for over two weeks. How will my body and soul respond to the incessant imitation of eventide which I know awaits me? I so want to feel "overwhelmed with joy" (Matthew 2:10), to kneel in homage at the recognition of something divine revealed in something so ordinary, and so feared. Yet a holy quest—be it for a child, or for darkness—renders the seeker vulnerable and carries with it great responsibility. To place preconceptions to one side and face the object of the search with an open heart and mind, to tell of the encounter with honesty and integrity—these things are paramount. So enthralled am I, and in love, with the condition of darkness, that I find it hard to imagine that a total immersion in it can be anything other than wondrous.

In Tromsø, where I stay en route, the hours between 10 a.m. and 3 p.m. are a kind of dusk, emanating a light which I associate with the ending of the day, a light that only lasts a short time, preceding the fall of evening. So it is strange to go out in the morning and find myself hurrying in anticipation of something which, in reality, is not to happen for a few hours to come—the descent of the fuller darkness. That sense of "wanting to get there before it gets dark" is something ingrained in us from childhood, particularly those of us who are part of a generation influenced by parents and grandparents who lived through at least one war, if not two, and experienced only nascent technology. The disorientation was compounded by the presence of a lighted candle on the table in the restaurant in which I ate my lunch at around one o'clock.

The Christ child is still in the crib in the chapel of "Totus Tuus", the Carmelite convent where I am staying en route to Svalbard. Until the festival of Candlemas he waits, apparently held in perpetual night-time (for we never imagine that scene during the day), testified to by the constant presence and illumination of the star above. Perhaps his sharing of the Polar darkness is a reminder of his presence at this time of year, when the more obvious and common symbols based on light and new life are absent. The Saviour of the world, grounded in the night-time of our childhood fantasies, is at home here, for this is not a time without purpose or meaning. Like the verdant growth held at bay beneath the frozen Arctic tundra, the child and his parents wait for a sign to come forth, using the time of shelter and gloom to prepare, to come to terms, to plan, to wonder, and to grow. In such a vision, we no longer see the child as the proverbial light of hope shining in the dismal darkness of the manger; rather, it is in the darkness of the stable that we see the child at his most fully human, at his most fragile and vulnerable, and filled with potential. At this point he can, like any child, become anyone or anything.

CHAPTER 1

The Visible Darkness

"Perhaps it would be a good idea if we . . . "

Richard stood in the doorway of the kitchen wondering how to arrange people round the table, but Brian quite misunderstood and said, "Draw the curtains. Jolly good idea. That's what we used to do for Sheila . . . pull the curtains to, you know, she liked the candles in the dark."

"Yeh," whispered Esther. "Yeh!"

While Eileen closed the curtains, Richard withdrew to the kitchen to light the candles without Esther seeing. The party fell silent in the half light, watching for the kitchen door to open . . .

Then the kitchen door opened and the cake and its magical lights floated towards Esther, whose eyes and hair shone with its flickering golden flames . . . A circle of eight flames to stare at in wonder and with awe.

*From **Skallagrigg** by William Horwood*[5]

I

My love affair with darkness began as a child. I recall a ritual performed by my mother who, every evening, would caringly leave a tea light at my bedside (although back then it was called a "night light"). It is one of those reveries that has assumed mythical proportions in my memory and it remains central to the joyful reminiscence of my past. That such an apparently inconsequential childhood routine could retain such potency in my adult imagination might be surprising, but we never know which fragments of the mundane will endure and shape who we become. Whether I had requested it, or whether my mother had simply assumed I would be afraid and brought it spontaneously, I really don't know. I certainly don't recollect that the dark held any particular terror for me. Yet I loved that night light and would wait expectantly for it. Not because the gentle light it shed made me feel safe but rather, I now realize, because it allowed me to see the dark. Not to see *in* the dark, but to *see* the dark. Somehow, instinctively, subconsciously I suppose, I recognized in the faint radiance of the small flame that it was the dimness itself which offered the restful, enfolding, reassuring experience, and that the depth of shade offered an ambience to be welcomed, not feared. It was the darkness, made visible by the light, that offered me peace, comfort, and rest, not the light itself. Forty years later, the street lights of Hackney, the neighbourhood of inner London where I live, and a twenty-four-hour urban sprawl create the effect of a technological moonlight. There is no need for a night light to illuminate the dark, even with the curtains closed. So the moment of the flick of the light switch is still a moment I long for, when the discomfort of fierce natural or artificial light on the eyes diminishes and the cathartic caress of the twilight leads me into the night. It is, as my young friend Tamsin told me with innocence, but great perception, when talking about her bedtime, "like turning the dark on".

What an insightful expression that is! With a childlike sense of wonder, it encapsulates an awareness that darkness is not to be feared, and that light is not about banishing darkness, but about opening up the possibility to live within darkness, of making a conscious choice to enter into it. It nudges us in the direction of being able to understand light not only as a means to enable us to see *in* the darkness but as a lens through which we see the darkness itself and are able to appreciate its particular qualities. In this way of thinking, light and dark become mutually dependent companions, like an elderly couple who have long since forgotten what it means to be independent beings, whose individual existences are so defined by their relationship to the other that life itself cannot be imagined in isolation, and when one dies the other quickly passes too, survival alone impossible to contemplate. Similarly, light and dark thrive off the energy of the other, only achieving the fullest possible significance when understood in relation to the other. When those ancient scribes, and their even more ancient story-telling ancestors, attempted in their scientific naivety to explain the natural phenomenon of the daily cycle of light and dark, they did not choose to take darkness away from the creative activity of God. Their narrative described God drawing light from darkness, akin to turning on some giant heavenly switch, offering equilibrium to the universe and placing both states at the mercy of humankind to do with what they would.

"It's like turning the dark on." That's a bit how I feel about the onset of autumn. And what's true for the end of the day is true for the end of the year—it can never come soon enough! The annual ritual of putting the clocks back one hour on the last Sunday in October is one I delight in, as the thought of early dark evenings begins to fill my mind, with the associated possibilities of snow days, hearty winter suppers, a quieter pace of life, and times of rest and recreation. The association with the season of Advent is also powerful—this mysterious time of waiting and preparation for God to come into the world; the world, ambiguously, into which God has already come. The darkness of the season seems somehow to echo the hidden presence of God at this time of year, whilst at the same time announcing God's self-revelation in the particular delights of winter and in the specific identity of the lengthening twilight-time. This stanza from the poem "Advent Calendar" by Rowan Williams captures the essence of God's manifestation in the diminishing light of December:

> He will come like dark.
> One evening when the bursting red
> December sun draws up the sheet
> and penny-masks its eye to yield
> the star-snowed fields of sky.[6]

So it happens then, usually by the middle of October, or perhaps earlier if the summer has been bright and warm, that I dare to articulate a sense of joyful anticipation at the impending changing of the hour. Always, however, I am greeted with incredulity, as if I were a child announcing that I was really looking forward to, and excited about, the start of my exams. "How could you *possibly* feel that way?!" The approaching darkness acts like a blue touchpaper to people's fears—both real and imagined—and despondency and anxiety can very rapidly set in, often exacerbated by the stresses of preparing for Christmas and New Year celebrations, or in the aftermath of the busyness, excitement, or anti-climax of them. So it feels like something of a confession to say that I prefer the autumn to the spring, the winter to the summer, and that at the end of the high season, I long for the clocks to go back and for the darker evenings. I yearn for these things much more keenly than I await the spring movement of the clocks in a forward direction; I love walking home surrounded by twinkling lights, the sense of promise and security offered behind closed doors, represented by the burning lights which rely for their warmth and glow on the darkness which envelops them. I cherish the sense of the darkness being vital to these experiences, the thing which gives life, in fact, to the light itself. I crave the sense of relief which the dimness of the evening offers at the end of a day—putting on a lamp rather than the main light, lighting a group of candles which have been lovingly arranged for maximum aesthetic impact, or simply turning down the dimmer switch. And just think for a moment of that brief, fleeting moment when you first put your head on your pillow at night, or whenever you sleep, and turn out the light; it doesn't last long but, just momentarily, there can be a sense of deep relief and peace.

It's a point which until very recently had passed me by, but the turning back of the clocks is, in fact, returning the clocks to the "right" time, Greenwich Mean Time, the official time in the UK since 1880. It was in 1916, during the First World War, that the idea of William Willett (a builder from London) to steal some daylight from the morning and shift it to the evening in the summer months was finally adopted as a means of saving fuel, and hence, money. Willett realized that in the summer some daylight hours are wasted because most people are still asleep in the morning. By taking some of that time and moving the clock forward, that daylight, he realized, could be used more effectively, offering more opportunity for daylight activity and delaying the need to turn on artificial lighting. The idea was taken up across Europe and America during the war, and although many countries abandoned the idea subsequently, the UK continued with the daylight-saving measures during the summer months. Over the years there have been various attempts to retain the "extra" hour of evening light throughout the year, and even to add an additional hour during the summer months, so that the UK would be one hour ahead of GMT in winter and two hours ahead in summer. Advocates of these suggestions quote reduced accident rates, energy-saving, and improved quality of life as reasons for changing. Opponents talk about difficulties posed by longer, darker mornings for farmers and schoolchildren and others who need to be alert and active earlier in the day. Whether light is most useful or best appreciated in the mornings or in the evenings is a question which can be answered both subjectively and objectively, and it is an agenda driven by political, economic, and sociological factors. A later chapter will grapple with some of the more complex political factors which come into play, particularly when extolling the virtues of darkness, and clearly there is a whole realm of practical difficulties which need to be overcome when the environment is dark. But for now, it is enough to observe that, however it happens, the changing of the hours appears to have as its underlying, unspoken agenda, the banishing of darkness; as long as time is manipulated in its present manner, come the end of summer, talk turns from holidays and barbeques and late but light outdoor living to the dread of the "clocks going back" and the associated closing-in of the evenings. When the change finally takes place, people scurry to get home before it gets dark and only venture out for evening activities with caution and reluctance. All this in spite of the capacity, which humankind has had for a long time, to be able to light up the darkness. In fact, human beings have been "turning the dark on" since around 70,000 BCE when prehistoric people discovered they could ignite moss soaked in animal fat held within a hollowed-out rock or shell. By 4500 BCE oil lamps were in existence and candles appeared about 1,500 years later. The rest, as they say, is history, and the apparent obsession with enlightening the environment is beautifully summed up in the final words of the German literary genius Goethe, "More light!"

II

The first reported public street lighting in Europe was as far back as the tenth century. Cordoba was the capital of Islamic Spain and one of the most populous cities of Europe at the time, a bustling multi-cultural metropolis, and its citizens were able to venture out in the dark on to their main streets under the glow of manually-lit kerosene lamps.[7] Technology has, of course, moved on in leaps and bounds since then and street lighting has undergone a host of various manifestations. In fifteenth-century Europe and Colonial America, lanterns were filled with tallow, fat, wax, and pith wicks. In 1667 Paris introduced a formal, if unsophisticated, system of public street lighting comprising little more than candles in jars. Two years later, Amsterdam followed suit but using a much more efficient oil-powered lamp. By the start of the eighteenth century, more than fifty of Europe's major towns and cities were lit at night. The early lamps were ignited manually by a "lamplighter" whose work began at dusk, but later more sophisticated designs allowed for an ignition device that would light a flame upon the activation of a gas supply. At the start of the nineteenth century, coal gas lamps were used, and by the end of the century electrified arc lamps and incandescent bulbs had appeared. In very recent times, a new and more energy-efficient street lighting technology has emerged: the solid-state light-emitting diode (LED), which has a hitherto unknown versatility as a source of light.[8]

Cultural historian Craig Koslofsky has written in detail about the more recent history of humankind's illumination of the night, particularly in Europe, and in his book *Evening's Empire*[9] he describes how the gradual move in seventeenth and eighteenth-century Europe towards lighting in public places, as well as the later invention and rapid spread of electric lighting, had a profound impact upon the way the time of day after sunset was viewed. With the day extended, the night became easier to use as a place of social, financial, and practical movement. Certain activities which had hitherto been impossible were made possible by being able to see *in* the night. People felt safer, their very practical concerns about falling on the poorly maintained and unhygienic streets dissipated. At the same time crime increased, not necessarily because of the darkness *per se* but because there were more people around, and hence more opportunities

for illicit activity. Socializing at night became more commonplace and led
to other associated sociological changes. For example, people started to
alter their appearance in order to look better in the night-time lighting,
meal times became later, and artists began to use the night to display
illuminations and fireworks.

Koslofsky has defined this significant period in the social and cultural
history of Europe as a "colonization" of the night. In other words, it was
a period when the night came under the regulation of humankind, and
became subject to its capacity to control and manipulate light and dark.
For certain wealthier sections of society it fashioned the opportunity for
displays of status and advantage. It created new opportunities for profit
and extravagance, although the emergence of a night-time economy
obviously created its victims and losers as well as its beneficiaries. If
human sleep patterns evolved as a result of the need to hide away from
night-time predators, then the opening up of the night as a legitimate
and safe space for activity and recreation meant that people could emerge
from the shadows and begin to define new patterns and ways of living.

In the modern world, night-time living is second nature for many.
Even those who prefer not to venture out after dark accept such activity
as the norm. It is not unusual or strange. People across the globe work
and play throughout the night and throughout the dark, some by choice,
some by necessity. It is possible that those first venturers into the night
hundreds of years ago, under the power of artificial light, thought that
what was happening was the beginning of the end of darkness. Influenced
by the strong associations of darkness with evil and menace that had been
commonplace for centuries, there would have been an entirely natural
optimism that the increasing power of human technology would be able
to rid the environment entirely of darkness, that it would push it away and
create an unending daytime, with uninterrupted illumination allowing the
activities of the daylight to continue unimpeded into the night. To some
extent such an assumption may continue to this day: an assumption that
the reason for lighting the night is to banish it, to get rid of it, to prevent
its associated difficulties from affecting us, simply to make the night easier
to use. We do not allow the end of daylight to stop us doing most things
we might want to do. As long as we have the appropriate artificial light we
can carry on uninterrupted. As I walk through the streets of London after

dark and glance up at the seemingly permanently lit office buildings, it is usually possible, no matter how late, to spy a lone worker, sat at a desk, frantically trying to meet a tight deadline for the following morning. Yet as much as modern lighting allows us to carry on after dark as if nothing had changed, the night-time does hold its own character; sometimes the late-night office worker is enjoying some peace and quiet, and the chance to concentrate in the absence of chatty, demanding daytime colleagues, or possibly taking refuge when the thought of going home is worse than staying at work. The night is different from the day.

It was the fourteenth of April, 1976. I had just turned thirteen and it was to be a day that I would remember all my life. Or rather, I should say, a night I would remember. I was already a devoted West Ham United supporter. For a couple of years I had been going to matches regularly with my brother, usually on a Saturday afternoon, but some games were played in the evening and this night was the biggest yet. I remember my bizarre costume, a large claret and blue rosette pinned into my hair, and my mascot, an old teddy bear which I had dressed in a miniature West Ham kit and whose paws I had embroidered with the club's logo. I was usually in a minority. A girl on the North Bank. Often the only one, really. But on that night, I found myself standing next to another, older girl who had long blonde hair and was wearing a black velvet jacket and one of those West Ham scarves that was mainly white rather than claret and blue. Such details! I didn't know her. I have never seen her again, as far as I know. It was raining. The muddy pitch deteriorated and the tension built. West Ham went from strength to strength (except for the last few minutes when all could have been lost) and my fellow-supporter and I embraced and jumped and cried together as our team beat the massive German side Eintracht Frankfurt and progressed into the final of the European Cup Winners' Cup. Even now, as I think of it, the Eagles' song "One of These Nights" comes into my head—I played it after I got home—and it certainly was one of those nights. One which epitomized the magical quality which all football fans will tell you is at the heart of any night-time football match. There is something which resists definition about the particular atmosphere generated, an atmosphere which I have no doubt is created not by the floodlights themselves, but by the darkness which they illuminate. It is the very *nightness* which draws the crowd together and creates a cocoon of solidarity and familiarity. Tucked together in the dark, like a family gathered around a hearth, sheltered but exposed. Forging from the shared passion and hope connections of deep but often fleeting intensity. Knowing that whatever happens we will be wending our weary way home at the end of the game, through the night, to continue with the mundanity of life beyond football. Many of those things are always there, at every game, but somehow the darkness intensifies the intimacy, and the floodlights lay it bare for all to see. Even today, when there are no terraces to jam us together and we have to sit in an orderly fashion, there is still something about the way the stadium creates its own world at night; the darkness drawing the voices together, magnifying the sound, and proving what everyone in the ground already knows to be true, that this is a mystical experience, a sharing of soul and spirit, not just a matter of life and death but, as Bill Shankly famously said, something far more important than that.

There is a side to the night which is not about fear or danger or lack of control, but about it being a unique space in which a particular atmosphere can be created and in which isolation and vulnerability are held in tension with festivity, peace, and inspiration. There is something about being able to enter into the night, or the dark, which moves us away from the routines and practices and emotions of the daytime and allows us to be different people. Or at least to explore diverse aspects of who we are. We dress differently, mingle with different people, engage in different activities, and feel differently. It is no accident that night-time is associated with creativity and the world of the artist and the young; it can be a truly inspirational time. More of that in Chapter 6! The onset of night-time and the turning-on of the lights allows us not simply to carry on as if nothing has happened, but to "see" the night for what it is—a unique time of day. Perhaps a gentler or more exciting time of day which moves us through recreation and into rest. A poetic and a seductive time, a time which draws us closer to one another and forces us to see things from an alternative perspective.

It is a harsh reality that in modern cities people are not familiar with the night sky. In spite of the "brave new world" which has opened up since streets and public spaces became artificially lit, there is a growing recognition of the impact of unnatural light upon our ability to see and recognize the stars and the countless other treasures which are held within the dark universe. An obsession with an illuminated world means that there is less of a need or tendency to look upwards and beyond, and even if we do allow our gaze to venture in that direction, what we see will be to a greater or lesser extent restricted, depending upon our proximity to an urban environment. From the point of view of a city centre, with its dense concentration of twenty-four-hour lighting emanating from street lamps and office buildings, floodlights and cars, and a whole myriad of different sources, the naked human eye, if it is lucky, might be able to see something in the region of one hundred stars.[10] The night sky is held in a permanent misty radiance—quaintly known as "sky glow"—with few distinguishing features other than, perhaps, the moon. This "sky glow" is created by lights radiating upwards and outwards, by illuminated objects reflecting light, and by misdirected and unshielded floodlights and security lights. In all of these instances, tiny specks of water or dust scatter the light in the atmosphere and cause the unrelenting glare with which we have become so familiar in the modern, urban context.[11]

Yet to move even a small way away from intense lighting, into a park or a garden, can increase visibility. Moving away from the city altogether, into a place where there is little or no artificial lighting, can increase tenfold the number of stars visible and it becomes possible to view the elusive Milky Way which, it is estimated, is only visible to around thirty per cent of the population of the US and Europe (eighty per cent worldwide).[12] In an attempt to recover some of the magic of the dark night sky, "Dark Sky Reserves" are being established across the world and the International Dark Sky Association recognizes places which, because of their low level of "sky glow", afford a clear perspective of the night sky. In such places, amateur and professional star-gazers alike can gather and view the universe unimpeded by the luminosity of modern technology. And in such phenomenal locations, it is impossible to escape the conclusion that it is too much light which stops us seeing the stars.

Some years ago, I was on the island of Iona, way up off the north-west coast of Scotland, with a group of students for the Iona Community's "Experiencing Easter" programme. Apart from the Christian Community based there, Iona has a resident population of about a hundred; there is no street lighting and anyone spending time there is urged to carry a torch once evening sets in. On the final night, returning home from the only pub on the island to our accommodation in the abbey, we found ourselves, for whatever reason, without a torch. Stepping outside, we felt temporarily blinded, disorientated, we couldn't see or make out a thing or focus on anything. We had to put our hands out in front of us to guide our way. But steadily, as we walked, our eyes adjusted and different shapes became apparent. Gradually we became able to see and—in a strange half-lit way—we realized that the sky was full of stars, the universe stretching out before us. It took our breath away, and we carried on past the abbey and walked a further mile to the shore, where we sat on the sand and watched shooting stars and satellites, trying to remember the names of the various constellations that were clearer than they had ever been. And we felt drawn into the embrace of God in every bit as real a way as if we had been standing on a mountaintop in broad daylight.

III

In allowing ourselves to "see" the darkness we become open to a fuller appreciation of the beauty of light and of the utter connectedness of the two states. A star without the deep blue sky at night is merely an inconceivably distant sun or planet, invisible to our eyes and unable to move us. A candle lit during daylight hours is just a burning pillar of wax, rendered purposeless, out of place, almost inappropriate. Here, AnneLise, who has lived in Svalbard for forty years, recalls a scene from her childhood:

> I've always been aware that light shines brightest in the darkness—
> we didn't have electric light until I was a few years old. The best
> part of the day was the hour or so before we lit the candles. Light
> doesn't have any power until there is a kind of darkness so it would
> be a misuse to light a candle and have it on the table when there
> was no need for it—that was the wrong use of the candles. But
> when it was dark enough we would light the candles. And in that
> hour before we lit them, there was just calmness, the stove was

warm and the cat was purring and my mother would be knitting
and we would be playing quietly—it was a twilight hour. Normally
doing nothing wasn't good, but in that hour we were supposed to
just relax and not do anything.[13]

In the natural world, there is no single, perceptible moment when light
becomes dark or dark becomes light. The remarkable but gentle change
from one to the other—when the relative qualities of light and dark are
held in tension and dusk renders the boundary between the two impossible
to trace—is a transition of infinite possibilities. However, at the first sign
of the natural daylight descending, the tendency in the modern world
is to turn on the electric light and to attempt to recreate the ambience
of the daytime so that activity and busyness can continue unhampered.
In many environments, electric lights burn throughout the day anyway
so the shift from afternoon light to evening light passes by unnoticed, is
rendered virtually invisible. For the one who can resist the light switch
and pause in these twilight moments to observe the subtle changes, the
rewards are rich. It is perhaps why, within the Arctic Circle, the few weeks
of the year which harbour both light and dark are revered and planned
for with such a great sense of anticipation. Whilst around the world,
wherever we live, we will have the same total number of daylight and
dark hours across a year, for those places where the distinctive periods
are experienced in lengthy, intense blocks, the joy of the transition time
is palpable. Here both light and dark are able, albeit briefly, to play with
one another, reflect each other, and rejoice in each other, the respective
qualities of each coming into full perspective when juxtaposed with the
other. We need the dark to help us see the light. A flame lights up the
dark, not to extinguish the dark or to overcome it, but that we might see
the dark more clearly.

Svalbard Journey
First Visit, 13 January 2013

How to describe the Northern Lights? It feels a fruitless exercise, because some things—like God, perhaps—should remain undescribed, held only in the treasure store of memory. Yet human instinct drives us to seek to share those things which move and fascinate us. Hence in the presence of beauty we weaken and take out our cameras and our pens, diminishing the experience but at least attempting to pass on a shred of it. In our drive to describe nature, as with our drive to describe that which is divine (if indeed these things are separate), the acceptance of the apophatic does not come naturally. So as I stand, minute and invisible, nestled between mountains and staring skywards, the immediate thing which occurs to me when the aurora appears is that I am witnessing the first act of creation, the moment when God brought forth light from the dark at the beginning of time. As the light seeps through the blanket of the dark sky, forming itself into magnificent and graceful shapes, I imagine God's delight, echoing my own and that of my companions, for it is as if we have never before beheld such a thing as this.

Another image places itself in my mind's eye. It is as if an army of torchbearers—themselves out of sight—are about to come over the crest of the mountain. A huge search party, but at this point with just their beams visible, swaying gently and randomly. Gradually the seekers ascend on the other side of the peak, putting their attention and energy into generating momentum forwards and upwards rather than concentrating at this stage on controlling the movements of their arms and the direction of their searchlights. The lights become larger and appear to be coming closer, but then they fade, and the explorers never appear; they are exhausted, perhaps, and beaten into retreat by the cold and the steep incline, or simply by the fruitlessness of their search. They take their lights with them.

It is as if wafts of translucent smoke are drifting up from campfires, shape-shifting and swirling in the sky before fading and blending into the darkness. Or a long, long bridal train caught in a gust of breeze is swept vertically upwards above the bride's head, becoming silhouetted against an empty sky before bending and falling softly back to earth.

When the aurora manifests itself as a single shaft, straight and uniform across the dome of the sky, it is as if the heavens have momentarily split open—just a narrow fissure—allowing the radiant spirits of a heavenly realm (whose colour is beyond description) to push their way through. And then it closes, like the gateway to Narnia, only to be opened at another unknown moment in time, beating the luminescents into retreat and once again shutting off the beauty of the earth from those above who would wish to glimpse it.

CHAPTER 2

The Sacred Darkness

I said to my soul, be still,
and let the dark come upon you.
Which shall be the darkness of God.

T. S. Eliot[14]

I

On the Wednesday of Holy Week I attended a Tenebrae service at an Anglo-Catholic church in central London. The word "*tenebrae*" is a Latin word meaning shadows or darkness. The service more usually takes place on Maundy Thursday evening, or on Good Friday, but its general setting at the heart of Holy Week gives it a particular emphasis which draws the participant into the Passion story with a dynamic emotional potency. Each Tenebrae service carries its own identity, but there are some common features. It is usual to start with the church lit by a few candles, normally as many candles as there are readings included in the liturgy, plus a white Christ candle. Psalms, canticles, and other readings reflecting the intensity of the Passion narrative are shared in word and song; when each reader has read a lesson, one of the candles is extinguished, until finally only the Christ candle remains. Eventually, as the story reaches its climax and Christ is led to his death, that final candle is put out, or removed, leaving the congregation in near darkness, save for any vestiges of daylight or strands of persistent, external artificial light which intrude into the building. It is pure theatre. Superficially, it might be understood that the darkness represents the suffering of Jesus on the cross and the moment of his death. Yet there is more to it than this. In the dark, all is laid bare, the tears can flow unnoticed, and the suffering of Christ which reaches its pinnacle at that point becomes perfectly connected with my own and that of the people of God throughout the millennia. The darkness does not represent the suffering, but rather becomes a holding place in which I can be truly myself. Nothing is hidden, and I can call out to God who has not forsaken me but meets me face to face.

Often, at this point the service ends. No benediction, and a silent departure. It is left unfinished because the story, of course, unfolds over the next few days. The desolation of the service is intended to intensify the joyful moment of the resurrection, and the use of darkness to connect people with the darkening of the earth, at the moment of the death of Christ on the cross, helps us to connect our own pain with the pain of Christ's Passion, so that the delight and hope of the resurrection can be experienced all the more fully. The darkness is not a symbol of death, but more of a reminder of the utter presence of God in that moment. It is that all enveloping, protecting darkness in which life is nurtured and love is made. In the space between Good Friday and Easter Sunday we are particularly able to discover the regenerative power of the darkness; Daniel O'Leary describes Holy Saturday—the day between Good Friday and Easter Sunday—as being a "dark space when the tomb becomes the womb . . . the time when Jesus was accomplishing his most precarious mission."[15] For us, it is from within the heart of that three-day state of nothingness that salvation emerges, in the One whose experiences authenticate our own death and pain, and whose delayed resurrection points to the necessity of darkness as a fundamental restorative state of the human condition.

The Tenebrae service I attended did not end with the darkness but rather included the return of the Christ candle, accompanied by a very loud noise intended to symbolize the earthquake at the time of the resurrection. For me, bringing the light back at that point took me prematurely and unwillingly into that otherworldly realm in which Christ is no longer a human like me but divine, resurrected. I was not allowed to dwell in that perfect darkness which connected me, the broken human being, to the God who is the darkness which heals. Christ no longer rested with me as a human companion but was thrust ignominiously into the world of the divine, resurrected far too suddenly and far too quickly. Like a 150-watt light bulb turned on suddenly in the middle of the night, inducing panic, temporary blindness, and disorientation, the return of the Christ light seemed to miss the truth, so beautifully described by Karl Rahner, that "all clear understanding is grounded in the darkness of God."[16]

II

The Neolithic communities within which creation myths were cradled and cultivated, and from which the accounts in Genesis eventually emerged, would have understood the mutual interdependence of the night and the day, as their primeval existence revolved naturally around the light-dark cycle. As more formal methods of agriculture began to develop from around 3500 BCE, the moon began to take precedence over the sun as a means of measuring the movement of time. No longer was a simple rhythm of night and day adequate. It was necessary to monitor time accurately over longer periods, and the reliability of the moon's waxing and waning offered a means of doing this which was not prone to the unpredictability of weather patterns associated with the movement of the seasons.

Calendars based on the lunar cycle evolved in many of the great ancient civilizations across the globe, including the Hebrew, Greek, and Babylonian, and the moon came to hold immense religious significance. In 1897, a lunar calendar dating back to the first century BCE was discovered in France. The Coligny Calendar, as it became known, used nights to mark the passage of time; months, years, and longer periods all fell into two distinct halves, characterized by light and dark. Each month reached an apex called the "*atenux*" (meaning "returning night")[17] preceded by the period from the new moon to the full moon—which marked the first half of the month—and followed by the period from the full moon back to the new moon—the second half. The darkest time (the new or crescent moon) was the "sacred starting point"[18] and the zenith of the cycle (the full moon or brightest time) was marked as the point when the darkness would begin to return (hence "*atenux*", or returning night).

In the same manner, the year was separated into two distinct parts, the winter/darker months which were described as "*mat*" (meaning good) and the summer/lighter months, described as "*anm*" (meaning bad).[19] The festival of Samain, which marked the time of the harvest and the start of winter, was a sacred time when crops would be gathered, and meat and other foods stored for the winter. Although food stocks dwindled as winter progressed, the ongoing sacred rites and religious rituals of this season were believed to offer protection and a promise of well-being. On the other hand, the festival of Beltain, marking the onset of the lighter half of the year, was accompanied by a sense of anxiety as to whether or not the forthcoming harvest would be fruitful. Grain stores from the previous harvest would have run out, but it would still be several months until the next harvest. Whilst this festival was somewhat carefree, a time for fun and feasting where possible, it was also considered necessary at this time of year to offer more sober rites of appeasement to ensure the ongoing safety of life in all its forms.

The Celtic Coligny Calendar's cycle of waxing during dark periods and waning during the light reflects a deep-seated and intuitive understanding of the balance of nature and society, and demonstrates that the contemporary dualistic association of light with goodness and dark with evil is not widely reflected in what is known of many ancient cultures. Perhaps it is not surprising, then, that the first biblical creation myth and other references to creation prioritize darkness, or at least place it on an equal footing with light.

III

The importance and sheer usefulness of darkness continues to play its part as the story of the people of God unfolds in the Hebrew Bible. In establishing a covenant with Abraham, God points Abraham towards the night sky, telling him that the stars are as many in number as his descendants shall be (Genesis 15:5), and it is after the sun has gone down (Genesis 15:17) that the specifics of the covenant are finally outlined. Later on, darkness is an important and powerful motif in the exodus from Egypt of the Hebrew people under the leadership of Moses. It starts at midnight, with God striking down all the firstborn children of Egypt, the Pharaoh's child included. Still in the night, Pharaoh summons Moses and finally, after 430 years of captivity, the Hebrew people are told to leave. There follows a frantic scene, the implication of which is that it is still dark, as the people scoop up their possessions, including bowls with unleavened bread, and flee into the night. It is described as "a night of vigil, to bring them out of the Land of Egypt" (Exodus 12:42). As the story unfolds, God puts darkness between the Egyptians and the Israelites in the form of a pillar of cloud and fire (Exodus 14:19–20), thus helping the latter to escape. Moses then encounters Yahweh in "the thick darkness" at the top of Mount Sinai (Exodus 20:21) where he receives various laws and instructions which are to govern the Israelites in their keeping of the Covenant with God.

The Old Testament is replete with poetic and positive dark-related images which offer a vision of God residing in the darkness. David's Song of Thanksgiving to God for deliverance from his enemies describes how God responded to David's cry and came down from heaven. We read that "thick darkness was under his feet" and "he made darkness around him a canopy" (2 Samuel 22:10, 12; echoed in Psalm 18:9, 11). Psalm 17 offers the night as a time of purgation, when God can visit us, try our hearts and test us: "If you try my heart, if you visit me by night, if you test me, you will find no wickedness in me; my mouth does not transgress." (Psalm 17:3). It is not an incidental feature of the Scripture, this emphasis on darkness as a gift, a sign of God and of God's shelter and justice. In the anointing of Cyrus, the Lord says, "I will give you the treasures of darkness and riches hidden in secret places, so that you may know that it is I, the Lord, the God of Israel, who calls you by name." (Isaiah 45:3). Psalm 121 equates shade with protection from evil, verses 5–6 saying, "the Lord is your shade at your right hand. The sun shall not strike you by day, nor the moon by night." Psalm 97 places the seat of God's righteousness in the darkness: "Clouds and thick darkness are all around him; righteousness and justice are the foundation of his throne." (Psalm 97:2).

One of the best loved and most widely known biblical stories is that of Jonah who, in trying to run away from what God is asking him to do, ends up being thrown overboard from a ship. God sends a large fish (the whale is only of our imagining!) which swallows Jonah and holds him there in contemplation and prayer for three days and nights. It is not made explicit, but the environment in which Jonah is held—in the belly of the fish—can only have been one of total darkness. It is in that darkness that Jonah encounters God most profoundly and experiences a transformation of heart and spirit. When he is finally expelled from the fish he has a new-found resolve to respond to the call of God upon his life to preach repentance to the people of Nineveh. As Jonah's story continues, after his release from the belly of the fish, God continues to use darkness as a device in the lessons God wants to teach Jonah. After the people of Nineveh have repented, having heard Jonah's cry to them, God forgives them and saves them from destruction. Jonah is angry with God, thinking that the Ninevites should have had their comeuppance! As he waits to see what will happen, God offers Jonah the shade of a bush "to save him from his discomfort" (Jonah 4:6). When God eventually kills the bush, the shade of which has protected Jonah and made him happy, Jonah is again angry as the sun beats upon him and threatens to kill him. God finally makes the point to Jonah that if he thinks God should have saved the bush, just because its shade protected him, then how much more should God have the right to save the people of Nineveh.

One of the best known and most frequently quoted dark-related images in the Old Testament is found in Psalm 139. In the context of a treatise about God's omnipresence and omniscience, we read in verses 11 and 12:

> If I say, "Surely the darkness shall cover me, and the light around
> me become night," even the darkness is not dark to you; the night
> is as bright as the day, for darkness is as light to you.

The writer here is describing the impossibility of hiding from God's presence, and the lyrical imagery which conceives light and darkness as mirror images of each other is used to convey the understanding that God's eye sees all things at all times. Even the darkness of night cannot be a hiding place. This is an ambiguous passage, though, essentially poetic rather than literal or doctrinal, but I do not read it as saying that darkness does not exist for God, or that light is supreme—rather that darkness is not a place in which God is, or can ever be, absent. If we enter into a dark space believing that we will escape, or be hidden from, the divine gaze, then we must think again. For in that place we will not be invisible, but will encounter a God who gathers us into the bosom of divine safety. The physical and the metaphorical definitions of darkness seem to be playfully juxtaposed. The (physical) darkness is not dark (fearful) to God. (Physical) darkness is as light (goodness) to God. God formed us in the physical darkness of our mother's womb, therefore the darkness is not an environment in which we need be fearful, or in which we can deny who we are, or hide from our true nature or feelings. Rather, it is a place of growth, spiritual formation, and sanctuary; a place in which God meets us at our most vulnerable. In the end, whether it is light or dark is immaterial—if darkness is like light then light must be like darkness. The paradox of their comparable yet distinctive characters serves to reveal much about the wisdom and power of the divine nature, as being one which discloses itself persistently and constantly. God's eye perceives humankind always and everywhere, and both night and day, and dark and light, can be harbingers of an intimate and reassuring presence. This extract from "The Changes in the Sky" by John Pulsforal effortlessly reflects the glorious revelation which is at the heart of Psalm 139:

> What is the lesson conveyed by the great alternate changes of the sky? Now it is sweetly luminous, and now a solemn darkness. Strictly speaking, as we all know, there is no change in the sky at all. It is always an infinite darkness, and always lit up by myriads of stupendous suns. But we should not know this if the earth did not turn on her axis, and successively face the sun, and again turn away from him. To the turning of our planet from the sun we owe our knowledge of the universe. In the symbolism of its darkness and light we have our sublimest revelation of God. Light which is called God, and is God, issues for ever from the Infinite Bosom of His darkness. Darkness and light are both alike to Him; for He is as much one as the other.[20]

None of this is to say that a negative usage of darkness is absent from the Hebrew Bible. Far from it! Even as God is using the cover of darkness to explain things to Abraham, the sense of fear and dread that the old man feels is described by the writer as being like a "terrifying darkness" descending upon him (Genesis 15:12). The ninth plague which the Lord sends upon Egypt is that of darkness (Exodus 10:21), although the repercussions of it are perhaps not quite as drastic as the previous plagues. In fact, one might think that a three-day enforced stay at home would be something of a relief after the preceding chaos of frogs, gnats, locusts, thunder, and hail! Having said that, there is no doubt that this is intended to be part of the overall punishment of Pharaoh for his treatment of the Israelites. The prophet Isaiah uses darkness as a metaphor for hunger and affliction (Isaiah 58:10), and in spite of describing how God created darkness, verses from 2 Samuel and Psalm 18 (2 Samuel 22:29 and Psalm 18:28) also describe God as the lamp who lightens the darkness. Psalm 44 laments God's covering of the people with darkness as an affliction (Psalm 44:19) and Psalm 82 equates darkness with ignorance (Psalm 82:5). At the same time that the Lord is proclaiming to Job that he was the one who made the darkness (Job 38:9), he is describing the use of darkness (or at least the withholding of light) as a punishment (Job 38:15) and as an analogy for death (Job 38:17, 19).

From Christianity's earliest known writings, darkness and night bore heavily negative connotations, with many writers equating darkness with sin and death. The writer of the Acts of the Apostles associates darkness with the power of Satan (Acts 26:18). In his letter to the Romans, Paul describes acts of "debauchery and licentiousness . . . quarrelling and jealousy" as works of darkness (Romans 13:12–13). Indeed, his letters overall (as well as those written in his name, and other epistles) abound with imagery which equates darkness with evil, punishment, and with the condition of being distant from God (Ephesians 5:8, 11; Colossians 1:13; 1 Thessalonians 5:5; 1 Peter 2:9; 2 Peter 2:17; 1 John 1:5, 6 and 2:8, 9, 11, for example). Such biblical associations have clearly influenced writers ever since, writers who in turn have influenced the popular imagination. Seventeenth-century writer John Milton's epic poem *Paradise Lost*, for example, imagines the flames of hell as a "darkness visible":

. . . But his doom
reserved him to more wrath; for now the thought
both of lost happiness and lasting pain
torments him: round he throws his baleful eyes,
that witnessed huge affliction and dismay,
mixed with obdurate pride and steadfast hate.
At once as far as Angels ken he views
the dismal situation waste and wild.
A dungeon horrible, on all sides round,
as one great furnace flamed; yet from those flames
no light; but rather *darkness visible*
served only to discover sights of woe,
regions of sorrow, doleful shades, where peace
and rest can never dwell, hope never comes
that comes to all, but torture without end
still urges, and a fiery deluge, fed
with ever-burning sulphur unconsumed.
Such place Eternal Justice has prepared
for those rebellious; here their prison ordained
in utter darkness, and their portion set
as far removed from God and light of Heaven
as from the centre thrice to th' utmost pole.
Oh how unlike the place from whence they fell![21]

Perhaps the most pervasive biblical imagery is that which is presented in John's Gospel (John 1:5; 3:19; 8:12; 12:35, 46), from which, arguably, the most enduring and influential Christian metaphor emerges—that of Christ as the "Light of the World":

> Again, Jesus spoke to them, saying, "I am the light of the world. Whoever follows me will never walk in the darkness but will have the light of life."
>
> ***John 8:12***

In spite of the relentless and mainly consistent use of darkness as a negative metaphor in the New Testament there are, however, a good number of events which take place in the darkness. These are events which offer, in some sense, hopeful and positive narratives of transformation and divine encounter. In Matthew's and Luke's Gospels, an angel communicates with Joseph in a dream, telling him of Mary's conception. Jesus is born at night and his birth is revealed to the shepherds and the wise men (who have followed a star to reach him) at night. Mary and Joseph's escape to sanctuary in Egypt, with a death threat hanging over the head of their newly-born child, takes place under the cover of night (Matthew 1:18–2:14 and Luke 2:1–14). In Mark's Gospel we meet Jesus healing in the dim light of sundown and praying in the deep darkness of early morning (Mark 1:32–39).

Even in John's dark-loathing Gospel, exciting things happen once the light has faded! In chapter 3 we meet Nicodemus, a learned teacher and scholar who comes to Jesus after sundown to seek answers and to expand his mind. A traditional interpretation of that text holds the darkness of the night as symbolic of Nicodemus's ignorance, contrasting with the "light" revealed in Jesus's discourse. However, it is the depth of night which offers the Pharisee the cover of discretion needed so as not to be seen consorting with one who might be considered an enemy. And in that meeting some of Jesus's most complex, obscure, and radical theology is revealed. The night apparently serves Nicodemus well, setting him off on a journey in which we see him let go of a purely rational way of thinking and embrace the more mystical path of Jesus. Henry Vaughan reflects upon this meeting in his magnificent poem, "The Night":

> Through that pure virgin shrine,
> that sacred veil drawn o'er Thy glorious noon,
> that men might look and live, as glowworms shine,
> and face the moon,
> wise Nicodemus saw such light
> as made him know his God by night.
>
> Most blest believer he!
> Who in that land of darkness and blind eyes
> Thy long-expected healing wings could see,
> when Thou didst rise!

And, what can never more be done,
did at midnight speak with the Sun!

O who will tell me where
he found Thee at that dead and silent hour?
What hallowed solitary ground did bear
so rare a flower,
within whose sacred leaves did lie
the fulness of the Deity?

No mercy-seat of gold,
no dead and dusty cherub, nor carved stone,
but His own living works did my Lord hold
and lodge alone;
where trees and herbs did watch and peep
and wonder, while the Jews did sleep.

Dear night! this world's defeat;
the stop to busy fools; care's check and curb;
the day of spirits; my soul's calm retreat
which none disturb!
Christ's progress, and His prayer time;
the hours to which high heaven doth chime;

God's silent, searching flight;
when my Lord's head is filled with dew, and all
His locks are wet with the clear drops of night;
His still, soft call;
His knocking time; the soul's dumb watch,
when spirits their fair kindred catch.

Were all my loud, evil days
calm and unhaunted as is thy dark tent,
whose peace but by some angel's wing or voice
is seldom rent,
then I in heaven all the long year

would keep, and never wander here.

But living where the sun
doth all things wake, and where all mix and tire
themselves and others, I consent and run
to every mire,
and by this world's ill-guiding light,
err more than I can do by night.

There is in God, some say,
a deep but dazzling darkness, as men here
say it is late and dusky, because they
see not all clear.
O for that night! where I in Him
might live invisible and dim![22]

Although the poem does present Christ in terms of light, this is not a light in opposition to darkness, but rather a light which needs the darkness in order to be viewed. Just as the "pure Virgin-shrine" is evocative of the Christ-child being carried in the darkness of his mother's womb, so the night shields Christ and allows Nicodemus to see him clearly.

The very same Nicodemus it is, now apparently operating openly as a friend of Jesus, who helps to bury Jesus's body quickly after his crucifixion, for it is after sundown, the Jewish Day of Preparation (John 19:39). It is in the darkness of the tomb that Lazarus (John 11:43–44) and Jesus come back to life, and in the dark dusk of morning that Mary Magdalene encounters the risen Lord (John 20:15–16). We traditionally think of the resurrection as being light in the darkness, yet God uses the cover of darkness in which to carry Jesus into new life: the darkness of Good Friday continuing into Holy Saturday and through into the resurrection moment which itself takes place in the darkness of night or the dimness of dawn. It is during the evening that Jesus first appears to his disciples, offering them peace and forgiveness and charging them to do the same (John 20:19–23). In this encounter, it is almost as if the darkness offers a protective veil, in which Jesus can reveal just enough of himself to show his wounds clearly, but without frightening his friends. It is in the first, dim light of morning that Jesus later appears to some of his disciples by the Sea of Tiberias and helps them to catch fish which they share together for breakfast (John 21:4–14).

The inconsistency between metaphor and reality in John's and, to a lesser extent, the other Gospels, seems to pass the writers by! In the darkness of night an epiphany and a conversation of potential life-changing significance take place; resurrection breaks through and the glory of God is revealed. Yet still, in the midst of these things, darkness continues to be used as a term to describe malevolence and the absence of God. "And this is the judgement, that the light has come into the world, and people loved darkness rather than light because their deeds were evil." (John 3:19).

Svalbard Journey
First Visit, 13 January 2013

It takes me half an hour to get dressed: a borrowed snowsuit, made for someone twice my size; special boots that seem to be half my own body weight in insulation and which pin me to the floor; some kind of Lycra balaclava with a nose mask, worn underneath the snowmobile helmet which had to be fastened on me, as if I were a small child being prepared by her father to go out and play in the snow. We set off, me precariously poised on the back of the scooter, never feeling more like a city girl, yet exhilarated by the speed, the darkness, and the intense cold which manages to find the few tiny gaps in my supposedly all-encapsulating clothing. Out of the town we ride, our small convoy, leaving the dim street lights behind and travelling into the abyss. Nothing but ice and snow in every direction, only the headlights of our vehicles to guide the way. That, and the knowledge of our guide, Swein, into whose hands I am about to place my life.

We arrive at the ice "cave", the destination for our afternoon adventure. The entrance is unlike that of any cave I have ever visited: a small hole, perhaps three feet high and wide, going directly downwards through the snow and ice. I think of the slide at the top of the Magic Faraway Tree, the only means of descent down through the trunk into the darkness. I need explanation and reassurance, and then before I know it I am sliding on my belly, albeit briefly, into the chamber below which opens out like a treasure trove as the lights from our torches catch the ice crystals and reflect on the stalactites and mysterious ice formations. I wish I could remember things I think I learned at school about glacial formation and ice movement. Somehow we are beneath the glacier, deep inside the earth, and we walk and crawl and marvel until we finally settle in an inner chamber and turn off our torches. This is perhaps the only sort of place where it is possible in natural conditions to achieve total blackness. Normally in such acute darkness the eyes will gradually adjust, and after a period of time be able to see something, shapes and forms at least, if not detail. Yet here, after many minutes, I hold my gloved hand in front of my face, barely an inch away, and only the feel of my breath upon it tells me that it is there.

There is fear, but utterly unconnected with the darkness, more to do with a slight claustrophobia, although I feel great trust in my guides, and my sense of the awesome weight of ice above soon dissipates. And as we sing in Norwegian, Swedish, English, and Greek ("Amazing grace", "Alleluia", "Kyrie eleison" to name a few of the songs we sing) with only the sound to connect us, I reflect that this would not be the worst way I could die. And anyway, if this is what it is like in the grave, it was surely in such darkness that Christ came back to life.

CHAPTER 3

The Mystical Darkness

Joyful is the dark,
Holy, hidden God,
Rolling cloud of night beyond all naming:
Majesty in darkness,
Energy of love,
Word-in-flesh, the mystery proclaiming

Brian Wren[23]

I

Some of the most spectacular of all the gardens owned by the English National Trust are those at Stourhead, nestling just off the A303, in deepest rural Wiltshire, a short distance from the ancient monument of Stonehenge. The gardens, which cover more than 1,000 hectares, are set over several levels and contain within them a vast variety of species and styles. They are full of spectacle and mystery, and in fact, if you take a guided walk, you will be informed early on that the playful principle of the garden's design is "conceal, reveal, surprise". The unique layout, carefully planned and planted, means that the explorer might be walking along a particular pathway, only to turn a corner and realize that the wooded glen which had been casually and indifferently passed by, actually—from a different angle—contains a peculiar folly or a remarkable tree. The sudden revelation leads to a sense of wonder and surprise which would have been missing had the object revealed been placed in full view from the outset. That which had been hidden from sight is exposed in all its glory, offering an enchanting and mystical experience to the curious visitor. When I first walked the gardens at Stourhead it was pouring with rain, but having travelled a long way and being accompanied by a friend who had travelled even further, I determined to see it through, thinking we could make a cursory exploration and then head for cover. That was before we were captivated by the notion of "conceal, reveal, surprise" and found ourselves drawn into the enigmatic anticipation of a spirited exploration which somehow rendered us oblivious to our increasingly dampened state. The excitement and capacity for endurance came, for me, in the realization that in "conceal, reveal, surprise" I was encountering a powerful Trinitarian metaphor, in which the revelation of the Son and the surprise of the Spirit only hold meaning and potency in the company of the God, the One, who is concealed or (we might say) who dwells in darkness.

Whilst there is a certain inconsistency within biblical writings when it comes to the use of darkness as a metaphor or narrative device, by the fifth century CE, darkness and night began to emerge—particularly within the tradition of Greek mystical theology—in ways which were more consistently suggestive of a positive pathway to a divine encounter. Very influential here was Dionysius (or less glamorously, Denys, also known as the Areopagite) who, writing around this time, began to associate darkness with the transcendence of God. He wrote that, "the mysteries of God's Word lie simple, absolute and unchangeable in the brilliant darkness of a hidden silence."[24]

Although written much later, Henry Vaughan's poem "The Night", referred to in Chapter 2, draws on Dionysius's image of a brilliant darkness—and helps us to understand it—in his reference to a "deep but dazzling darkness". Such a brilliant or dazzling darkness hints at the night-time as a place of intense spiritual impact. In the darkness, stripped of all that is superficial and distracting, it is possible to achieve a profound clarity of insight. Looking back at the poem for a moment, it is in the night in which Christ's "still, soft call" (stanza 6) can best be heard. Paradoxically, it is in the depth of night (the "stop to busy fools" referred to in stanza 5) that the human mind can be most spiritually alive.

Writers such as Denys and others (Gregory of Nyssa and Maximus the Confessor) take us on a journey into the apophatic; that is to say, into a place in which God is concealed, a place in which God can only be known in a recognition of God's unknowability. In such a theology, darkness becomes a metaphor for the state of encountering God which goes beyond all experience or knowledge or language. Writing more recently, Dionysius's namesake Denys Turner places the epic myth of the encounter between Moses and Yahweh on Mount Sinai alongside Plato's "Allegory of the Cave" (which tells of the ascent of the philosopher Socrates to wisdom) as the two primary narratives from which Western Christianity's ownership of the metaphors of light and darkness in the mystical praise of God emerged.[25] In reflecting upon the role played by the stories from Exodus and Plato, Turner says:

> In both the Allegory and in Exodus, there is an ascent towards the brilliant light, a light so excessive as to cause pain, distress and darkness: a darkness of knowledge deeper than any which is the darkness of ignorance. The price of the pure contemplation of the light is therefore darkness . . . but not the darkness of the absence of light but rather of its excess, therefore a "luminous darkness". In both, descent from the darkness of excessive light is return to an opposed darkness of ignorance . . . Light is darkness, knowing is unknowing, a cloud, and the pain of contemplating it, is the pain of contemplating more reality than can be borne.[26]

Dionysius (to stop us getting confused with the other Denys) wrote in Chapter Three of his work *Mystical Theology*, "the more we take flight upward, the more our words are confined to the ideas we are capable of forming; so that now as we plunge into the darkness which is beyond intellect, we shall find ourselves not simply running short of words but actually speechless and unknowing."[27]

Speechless and unknowing, yet by implication closer to the heart of the Divine, who is indefinable, enigmatic, unutterable, unimaginable, and ultimately, unknowable. Thanks to the formative writings of Dionysius, the metaphorical language of darkness and night emerged within Christendom, offering a vocabulary to help the mystic describe that which had hitherto been indescribable.

However, it wasn't to last! In the medieval period, the night once again became associated with menace and evil. Narrative poems such as "Beowulf" and "The Dream of the Rood" are characteristic of what Chris Fitter has noted are medieval texts which, with their emphasis on the night as a context full of danger and violence, are unable in any sense to offer a positive vision of the night.[28] In the specifically Christian Benedictine tradition, the work of Anselm of Canterbury (1033–1109) is rich in its use of imagery connecting light with God, but is utterly devoid of any positive darkness metaphors. Even the Benedictine communal night prayer—in spite of being understood as a nocturnal encounter with God—was believed to stand in resistance to the perils perceived to be abounding in the night. Frustratingly, and as a sign of the times, the influence of Dionysius's writing about darkness paled into insignificance compared to that of his writing about ecclesiastical hierarchy![29] It wasn't until a resurgence of interest in mystical theology in the fourteenth and fifteenth centuries, with mystics such as Meister Eckhart and the unknown author of the classic "Cloud of Unknowing", that an alternative to the commonly held perception of the night and darkness as being associated with evil could once again be articulated.

Probably the most significant shift, however, in terms of the use of darkness as an experiential and metaphorical pathway to God, came about as a result of the Reformation and its handmaid, the Enlightenment. The contemporary Catholic Franciscan priest and writer Richard Rohr has pointed out that the advent of Protestantism brought with it what he describes as a "necessary critical mind".

Rohr writes:

> Protestantism emerged around the same time as the invention of the printing press and also, in the next centuries, the Enlightenment. What has marked Protestantism from the beginning is a beautiful but almost neurotic need for certitude, ending up in redefining biblical faith with little knowledge of the older tradition of darkness, of not knowing, of *unknowing* and silence. Everything was a theology of light, clarity, order, certitude. So much so that Protestantism came to think it had a right to certitude . . . Faith

got defined in a very western, left-brain, verbal way that had
almost no space for mystery.[30]

Inevitably, in a period of history characterized by dualism, polarization,
and division, the straightforward imagery of light and darkness as good
and evil respectively was easily absorbed into the consciousness of those
at the forefront of the Reformation struggle. Very quickly that struggle
became defined in terms of darkness and evil on the one side, and light and
good on the other. Each side staked a claim to the "light" of right thinking
and theology, and rejected the "darkness" of ignorance, heresy, and evil
perceived in the alternative position and practice. Martin Luther—who
used the image of darkness to describe the failure of those who could
not accept what he believed to be patently obvious—was described in
a poem written in 1523 by Hans Sachs as a "Nightingale", whose song
would wake people from the night and call them to the "light of day".[31]
However, ironically, it was the polarization at the heart of the Reformation
schism which ultimately led to the possibility for darkness and night to
re-emerge as serious players in the canon of positive Christian metaphor.
By the end of the sixteenth century, in the immediate turbulent aftermath
of the Reformation, many groups were needing to meet in secret. There
were numerous confessions, all heretical to each other, and who or what
was to be labelled as evil or good was no longer clear-cut. Frequently-
shifting patterns of church establishment meant that a group which had
been *part* of the establishment could suddenly find themselves at odds
with it—certainly alienated from it, potentially persecuted by it. Under
the cover of night such estranged Christians would gather to worship,
and a perceptual shift took place: the night was no longer the time and
the place for witchcraft and things associated with the Devil and evil in
general, but rather it was an environment offering acceptance and safety
and freedom of speech. Thus were the doors opened—more widely than
ever before in the Christian era—for a spirituality to emerge which was
able to embrace darkness and night in all their mystical and divinely
orientated splendour.

Writers around this time began, once again, to use the night as a
potent, positive metaphor, and by the start of the seventeenth century
mystics, poets, and theologians were able to express a renewed sense of

the value of darkness in Christian culture, spirituality, and literature. By 1640, a dictionary of mystic theology[32] was offering definitions for several dark-related terms. As well as "night", there were entries for words such as "midnight" and "dusk". Interestingly, there was no definition for "day". Of particular importance around this time are the mystical theology of the Carmelite friar John of the Cross (1542–91), whose writings were first published in 1618, well after his death, and the writings of John Donne (1572–1631), whose spectacular prayer is still used to this day as a prayer of committal at a burial:

> Bring us, Lord our God,
> at our last awakening,
> into the house and gate of heaven,
> to enter into that gate,
> and dwell in that house,
> where there shall be
> no darkness nor dazzling,
> but one equal light;
> no noise nor silence,
> but one equal music;
> no fears nor hopes,
> but one equal possession;
> no ends nor beginnings,
> but one equal eternity;
> in the habitation of your glory and dominion,
> world without end. Amen.[33]

John of the Cross was inspired to extol the virtues of the night after escaping prison under the cover of a moonlit night. The night—both as a metaphor and as a real state—was to become the very foundation of his theology, and his escape became symbolic for him of the quest for unity with the Divine. His poem, "Dark Night", presents both a lyrical account of his escape and a summary of his complex theology, which focuses on the journey of the soul on a spiritual road in pursuit of a perfect union with God, a union which can only be achieved by "going forth in the dark and with yearnings of love".[34] Here is an extract from that poem:

One dark night,
fired with love's urgent longings
– ah, the sheer grace! –
I went out unseen,
my house being now all stilled.

In darkness, and secure,
by the secret ladder, disguised,
– ah, the sheer grace! –
in darkness and concealment,
my house being now all stilled.

On that glad night,
in secret, for no one saw me,
nor did I look at anything,
with no other light or guide
than the one that burned in my heart.

This guided me
more surely than the light of noon
to where he was awaiting me
– him I knew so well –
there in a place where no one appeared.

O guiding night!
O night more lovely than the dawn!
O night that has united
the Lover with his beloved,
transforming the beloved in her Lover.[35]

In two commentaries on the poem written by John himself, he compares the soul's journey towards a state of union with the Divine with three stages of night-time. The first part of the night is the time of nocturnal prayer when the distractions of the day (light) diminish and God becomes more recognizable. It is an introspective time, a time when the senses are heightened, a time of self-denial and increased self-knowledge, an ascetic time, the time which John called the "dark night of the soul" or the "dark night of the senses". The second part of the night, the "dark night of the spirit", is compared to midnight, the darkest part of the night. It is an apophatic time, a time for faith, when in total darkness the soul relinquishes the capacity for understanding and vision so that it can be closer to God. George Herbert describes this stage beautifully in his poem "Even-song":

> But Thou art Light and darkness both together:
> if that be dark we cannot see,
> the sun is darker than a Tree,
> and thou more dark than either.
>
> Yet Thou art not so dark, since I know this,
> but that my darkness may touch thine,
> and hope, that may teach it to shine,
> since Light thy Darkness is.[36]

And writing somewhat later, the Anglican minister Anthony Horneck (1641–97) said:

> Now is the soul nimbler, subtler, quicker, fitter to behold things sublime and great . . . Midnight prayers strangely incline God's favour.[37]

The third stage, the mystical stage, is compared to that point of night which is close to day. It is the time when, in solitude and utterly separated from thought and experience, the soul can find union with God. Lover and beloved become one in the dark and restful night of faith.

By the end of the seventeenth century, the shift in perception from pre- and early Reformation times is complete. Light and dark are no longer merely symbols or metaphors in opposition, polar opposites conflicting and competing for supremacy. Rather, they have become existential and tangible, co-dependent, balanced yet contrary. As Craig Koslofsky puts it:

> For light to exist, there must be darkness; and to know light, one must know darkness, because they are coexistent, not in

a relationship of presence and absence, but as complements to one another.[38]

Koslofsky has written a fascinating and incredibly detailed account of the way in which darkness has, at various points in the history of Christianity, been either loathed or lauded, and any reader wishing to explore these ideas in more detail is urged to look at this work, presented in his book *Evening's Empire: A History of the Night in Early Modern Europe*.[39] Suffice to say, the journey of darkness has been a turbulent one, and more recent times have once again seen the demise of darkness as a pathway to God. As night-time has evolved into a time of play and work, rather than a time of mystery and contemplation, ideas have once again shifted. Spiritually speaking, it is my perception that theologies of "unknowing" which embrace a mystical pathway to God are maligned as demonstrating a lack of faith. In the present day, there is a tendency among some Christian traditions to pursue a narrow and conservative theology which advocates certainty and literalism (manifested, for example, in the creationist movement). It can be argued that this has led to a pervasive dismissal of the radical contemplative path as being incoherent and heretical. Light and dark are once again finding themselves cast as the symbolic opponents in a great battle for the soul of humanity, and the still, small voice crying in the dark wilderness is straining to be heard. But heard it will be.

II

Walking into the outer precincts of the magnificent Sree Meenakshi Hindu Temple in Madurai in South India is an assault on the senses like no other. The heady fragrance of the jasmine flowers being sold to adorn the hair of the female devotees and the shrines of the gods, joined with the aroma of incense mingled with sweat, and the chaos and noise of a marketplace, all combine to create an intense atmosphere which is at the same time both fervent and calming. The shady light, which diminishes even further as one is drawn towards the inner sanctum, offers a welcome relief from the intensity of the noonday heat and humidity.

For many people, it is the festival of Diwali—the Festival of Lights—which is most strongly associated with the Hindu religion. The festival celebrates the story of Prince Rama and his wife Sita—it tells of Rama's courageous slaying of the Demon King Ravana and the rescue of his beautiful bride. In celebration, so the story goes, the gods showered flowers from the sky, and the people lined the streets with flags and garlands and lit oil lamps along the road in order to guide Rama and Sita safely home. In every dwelling an oil lamp was put in the window to welcome them back. To this day oil lamps are lit in Hindu households as part of the festival, as this great narrative is recalled and celebrated. For Hindus, it is a story of good triumphing over evil, and of light challenging the darkness and overcoming it. In the Rig-Veda, one of the most important of Hindu scriptures, the god Surya "is the sun of the heaven and his name is derived from the word 'svar' (light) . . . It is his work to dispel the dark night of ignorance and to dispense the light of life and health."[40] In the Upanishads the word "*Atman*", which is used to define the essence of humanity, means "shining" or "opposite to darkness". However, in spite of the importance given to light in Hindu culture and tradition, there is a sense in which darkness also plays a significant, central role. Anat Geva and Anuradha Mukherji describe how the traditional design of the Hindu temple is intended to draw the pilgrim into a physical darkness as a way of enabling a connection with the Divine:

> According to the Hindu faith, when a worshipper is in the presence of the divine, there should be nothing to distract his/her senses, including vision, and God shall reveal himself to his devotee gradually. Therefore, the innermost sanctum of the temple is shrouded in total darkness and the progression into the temple is a ritual movement where the devotee goes through the dynamic experience of the darkening spaces before reaching the darkest sacred chamber. This treatment of light ensures that by the time the pilgrim reaches the innermost chamber (*garbhagriha*) his/her eyes slowly become accustomed to the darkness and his/her state of mind befitting worship and is no longer plagued by worldly

thoughts. During this journey, one passes through many doorways, colonnaded halls and corridors, which are decorated with sacred carvings. These sacred symbols have a profound impact on the mind of the devotee; they simulate the mystery that envelops the universe and the divine spirit that illumines the universe. Reaching the holy sanctum, the worshipper enters a place for individual self-realization and personal relation with the divine. This sanctum is not intended for mass prayer or congregational worship. Thus, a basic premise can be drawn: the design of the Hindu Temple accommodated the faith which requires a procession toward the "holy darkness" and enhanced the spiritual experience.[41]

Darkness is also a key feature in the depiction of some Hindu deities and integral to their philosophical conception. The deity who first comes to mind is Kālī, the dark goddess of both destruction and renewal, who elicits as much ecstasy of love from devotees as awe at the violence she wields to cleanse the world of evil. Another deity who commands perhaps even more adherents is an avatar or incarnation of the god Viṣṇu. Kṛṣṇa (or Krishna) is portrayed as blue in colour, his name coming from the Sanskrit adjective *kṛṣṇa* (कृष्ण), which means black, dark, or dark blue. In the Brahma-Saṁhitā, a collection of prayers offered by Lord Brahmā in devotion to Kṛṣṇa, he is described as being "the colour of a fresh black cloud, although his bodily features are more beautiful than millions of Cupids". It is likely that aesthetic, etymological, or artistic factors were at play as Kṛṣṇa's depiction in art evolved, leading to the more popular and easily recognizable representation in blue that many people will be familiar with today. There may even have been some racist (or, more specifically, casteist) influence as darker skins were associated with lower castes, meaning that it would have been unthinkable to portray a divine being with dark skin. Interestingly, that paradox of portrayal can be precisely what makes the darkness sacred in this context, as it symbolically affords divine status to those who are marginalized and oppressed. The goddess Kālī (consort of Śiva), however, is the deity who embodies most significantly the significance of dark skin tone in the Hindu pantheon. The name Kālī (from the Sanskrit *kāla*, काल) has origins that variously denote black, dark-coloured, and black night. She is usually represented with a black skin tone, and her frequent portrayal as an aggressive, fearsome demon-slayer belies a more complex series of understandings which see her revered as a symbol of Brahman. Brahman is described in the Upaniṣads as "existence, consciousness, and bliss" (in Sanskrit *sat-cit-ānanda*), and in Hindu philosophy—as complex and multi-faceted as it is—Brahman is generally understood as an indescribable, transcendent, and ultimate reality. It is this interpretation of Kālī which is reflected in and by her physically dark complexion. The Mahānirvāṇa *Tantra* describes it thus: "Just as all colours disappear in black, so all names and forms disappear in her." Kālī is both the creator and the destroyer, her very darkness reflecting the infinite cycle of nature and the fundamental elements of the universe. As well as being the harbinger of divine wrath, she is also revered as a compassionate and caring mother goddess. Sri Lankan Hindu writer Romesh Jayaratnam describes Kālī like this:

> Often situated on the margins of high Hinduism, she remains much sought after by those in distress. Her petitioners include women and men in all walks of life, throughout the Hindu world, be it in Bangladesh, India, Nepal, Singapore, Sri Lanka or elsewhere. Kali negates conventional day to day morality and responds to the instinctive pleas of the dispossessed, the sidelined and victims of injustice. She is the solace for those who have no option where all else has failed. In short, she is the last resort for a person in need of a respite during the harsh trials and tribulations of life.[42]

For Ramakrishna, a nineteenth-century Bengali priest and mystic, the idea of the Ultimate Mother was synonymous with Kālī and darkness:

> My Mother is the principle of consciousness. She is *akhanda satchidananda*—indivisible Reality, Awareness, and Bliss. The night sky between the stars is perfectly black. The waters of the ocean depths are the same; the infinite is always mysteriously dark. This inebriating darkness is my beloved Kali.[43]

The same contradictions that exist within the Christian tradition are present within others too! Whilst darkness is both a representation of all that is bad in the world, it can at the same time hold deep significance as a symbolic and material pathway to godly encounter.

Buddhist mythology reveres a range of goddesses, many of whom are defined generally as "night goddesses". These spiritual guides and teachers, with their symbolic association with darkness, lead the pilgrim along the apophatic, invisible, and unknown path to enlightenment. Of particular interest is the goddess Tārā, who holds a special place in Tibet, Nepal, and Mongolia. Tārā, whose name can be considered to mean "star", is, in her green manifestation, associated with the night, that is, darkness. Tārā can also mean "one who redeems". Green Tārā's virtues are activity and compassion and she is balanced by White Tārā, who is associated with the day.

Even within Islam, in which the archetypal association of darkness with all that is bad and evil is traditionally strong, there is evidence of a contrariety which holds light and dark in perfect balance. In the Qu'ran, Surah 31 (Luqman) verse 29 says, "Did you not note that God merges the night into the day, and He merges the day into the night, and that He has commissioned the sun and the moon, each running to an appointed term", and Surah 36 (Ya-Sin) verse 40 says, "The sun is not required to overtake the moon, nor will the night precede the day; each of them is swimming in its own orbit."[44] The Islamic belief that Allah created all things in pairs (Qu'ran 51:49) has at its heart the sense of a balanced universe in which the dark of night offers the gifts of rest and stillness and the daylight the gifts of vision and reckoning.

However, it is within the tradition of Taoism that contrariety truly comes into its own. Most people are familiar with the notion of "The Force"—although sadly perhaps they are more familiar with the Jedi version of it than the Tao version! When Luke Skywalker's father went over to the "Dark Side" of the Force and became Darth Vader (perhaps the ultimate in "dark-evil" characters in popular Western culture) it was a straightforward shift from "good" to "bad". Whilst George Lucas, the director and writer of the *Star Wars* films, did apparently draw from Taoism in his definition of "The Force", some crucial and significant differences remained. For the Jedi (a made-up religion, in spite of 0.31 per cent of respondents in the British census of 2011 self-defining in this way!), "The Force" represents a simple dichotomy of good and evil, represented by light and dark. In Taoism, however, the two sides of the force, light and dark, do not denote good and evil but are rather intended to embody the balance at the heart of the universe. Too much of either can be a source of imbalance and lead to disharmony. The iconic symbol of Taoism—the intertwined black and white teardrops of *yin* (dark) and *yang* (light) with each teardrop containing a small circle of the other—is hugely significant. It is a universally popular symbol and is recognized widely although, a bit like the Christian symbol of the cross, it is not well understood. The symbol conveys the heart of the ancient Chinese philosophy: two opposing forces that are mutually dependent. That these forces are the very essence of the natural world is represented in the symbol by the fact that the *yin* and *yang* link perfectly together and in their connection form a complete circle. The life of the individual is thrown into disorder and disarray if these two forces are not held in perfect equilibrium because the natural order of the universe becomes fractured.

René Guénon, the French metaphysician, explains that *yang* and *yin* "are associated symbolically with light and darkness; in all things the light side is *yang*, the dark side is *yin* . . . in the domain of manifestation, *yang* is never without *yin*, nor *yin* without *yang*."[45]

Svalbard Journey

First Visit, 10 January 2013

The magnificent mountains which loom majestically above Longyearbyen—which I have only seen in outline and in shadow— put me in mind of the biblical epic which takes Moses to the top of Mount Sinai where he encounters Yahweh in "the thick darkness". The resonance of a metaphorical darkness (as the place where God dwells) in a perpetually physically dark environment is potent. It makes sense. The unknowability of God in such harsh surroundings may be more obvious and easily understood than in a place of warmth and light, warmth and light being more readily acceptable and recognizable metaphors for the presence and "knowability" of God. Ultimately, though, what the unremitting darkness can teach us is to have confidence in the power of that unknowability, and to have faith that unknowability is not the same thing as absence.

CHAPTER 4

The Sublime Darkness

Deep into that darkness peering, long I
stood there wondering, fearing,
Doubting, dreaming dreams, no mortals
ever dared to dream before

Edgar Allen Poe, The Raven

I

In common parlance, the word sublime is used to describe that which is blissful and gorgeous, luscious and sensual. From a mouth-watering dessert, for me laced with liqueur, lime, and coconut, to an intimate personal encounter, use the adjective "sublime" and the listener or reader is left in no doubt as to the nature of the speaker's experience. It's also one of those words, the sound of which affords a particular rhetorical effect; it has an onomatopoeic quality about it. The thesaurus takes us in a slightly different definitional direction, towards that which is magnificent, inspirational, awe-inspiring, and transcendent. In either case, however, we are left with powerful positive images that evoke a sense of the Divine and leave the body breathless and the mind intrigued. It is within such an etymological framework that I would use the word "sublime" to describe many experiences of darkness.

The worlds of philosophy and art, however, have emphasized a specific tradition of "the Sublime" within which darkness is equated with destruction and cataclysm. Edmund Burke, in his seminal work *A Philosophical Enquiry into the Origin of Our Ideas of the Sublime and*

Beautiful (1757), argues that darkness has an inherently terrifying quality about it and is therefore strongly associated with, even a source of, the sublime. He describes the sublime as being "productive of the strongest emotion which the mind is capable of feeling".[46] He goes on to explain his understanding that pain and danger are stronger emotions than pleasure because they are emissaries of death, and that terror, therefore, becomes the "ruling principle of the sublime".[47]

Burke's *Philosophical Enquiry*, and the idea that sublime pleasure can only be reached after initial terror, was to have a lasting and profound impact upon British art in the late eighteenth and nineteenth centuries. The depiction of the insignificance of the human in relation to the magnitude and overwhelming character of the natural world became commonplace. This depiction frequently, if not normally, became characterized by darkness and a foreboding, brooding aesthetic quality. Menacing, epic scenes of natural disaster, devastation, isolation, and wrath—often rooted in biblical narrative—came to be depicted in shadow, in the darkness, and have served ever since in a wider context to underpin the association of darkness with that which is destructive. The equating of darkness with terror and devastation is a defining characteristic of the artistic movement of the sublime. There is no doubt that artists of this movement have used, and continue to use, a visual darkness as a means of conveying and underpinning the idea and the emotion of fear. Yet, as a friend of darkness, I find myself needing to ask the question: is darkness inherently to be feared? Or, in other words, is there an innate human response to darkness—which goes beyond inconvenience and sightlessness— that means it is irrevocably linked to despair? The seventeenth-century philosopher John Locke thought not, arguing in his "Essay Concerning Human Understanding" that "though great light be insufferable to our eyes, yet the highest degree of darkness does not at all disease them".[48] Burke argues, however, that "in utter darkness it is impossible to know in what degree of safety we stand",[49] and darkness, therefore, carries within it an innate quality of terror.

My instinct is that most people would stand with Burke on this one. The dread of the onset of winter and of dark places is a very real and present phenomenon in the lives of many people; it can be rationalized, articulated, and defended and it manifests itself in particular behavioural patterns intended to minimize contact with dark situations. The metaphorical association of darkness with death and fearful things is powerful, historically, sociologically, and theologically. Whilst for most people this association is held in control and can be approached with a degree of objectivity, for a few it becomes all-consuming. There is even a name for it; nyctophobia (extreme fear of the dark) is a recognized phobia, typically experienced by children who develop an irrational fear during the night that something calamitous is going to happen to them. Usually this fear diminishes as the child grows older but sometimes it continues into adulthood and needs to be treated as any other psychological condition. Researchers undertaking a sleep study in Boston, USA in 2012 reported that they were surprised by the number of adults who admitted to having a night-time phobia, and the study concluded that an underlying fear of the dark might be a cause of insomnia or other related sleep problems.[50] There is a theory that natural evolution has left the human race with an instinctive fear of the dark, a hangover from times when our ancestors were hunted and many of their predators emerged at night.[51] But whilst the dark-negative association is strong, so strong, grounded in history and tradition, perhaps even in biology, and reflected in language, art, philosophy, psychology, and religion, I am still reluctant to accept it as irrevocable, and find myself taking the side of John Locke in his classic debate with Burke. The researchers in the Boston study believe that their findings are relevant in terms of new approaches to treating insomnia. If lack of sleep is related to a fear of the dark, then traditional insomnia treatments which encourage sufferers to leave a dark bedroom and go into a lit room would not be effective; rather, the underlying cause—a dark-related phobia—needs to be overcome directly by increased exposure to darkness rather than avoidance of it.

II

If you are lucky, you may find on display in the Tate Britain art gallery in London a painting called "The Deluge" by the eighteenth-century British landscape painter Jacob More. The painting is part of the Tate collection but inexplicably not on permanent display, although I was fortunate enough to encounter it a few years ago as part of a special exhibition about "Art and the Sublime". The exhibition was contained within a single room and I sat on the benches in the centre, waiting for my friend to arrive, surrounded by gigantic canvasses filled with the magnificent, epic artwork of John Martin, James Ward, and others. But it was a much smaller painting hanging high up on the wall in the far corner that initially caught my eye. From the place where I was seated, I was observing the painting at a distance, from low down, and from a peculiar, acute angle. It attracted my attention because it appeared to be an entirely black canvas with a single pinpoint of light emanating from a central position. The light shone and appeared to irradiate the corner of the room in which the painting was exhibited, but I was intrigued by the apparently plain darkness of the rest of the canvas. When my friend arrived, we walked over to the painting, and it was only at that point that its detail and subject matter became clear. Although the overall impression remained one of shadow and obscurity, an intense and monumental landscape was exposed, along with a variety of minutely detailed human and animal figures. "The Deluge" was revealed as a scene of biblical proportions, representing a story of universal significance found within many of the world's major religions—that of a great flood sent by God to destroy civilization as a punishment for humankind's impiety. As a few exhausted people flail and struggle in the flood waters to save themselves, one another, and their animals, the last (or first—it is not clear to me) vestiges of sunlight can be seen between the threatening, gloomy, lofty outcrops of land which dominate the scene. The viewer is left in no doubt that this is an event of earth-shattering significance.

More's enduring legacy is to be found primarily in his earlier landscape painting, particularly works portraying his native Scotland. "The Deluge", however, is believed to have been painted towards the end of his life, when his work had taken on a more theatrical quality, and—unlike some of his other paintings—not much has been written about it. That this particular painting was displayed as part of an exhibition connected to the movement of "Sublime" art suggests a particular interpretation: that this is a scene of cataclysm and chaos, the gloominess of the canvas suggestive of terror, undoubtedly intended to point the viewer towards the vastness of the destruction and the inevitability of death. Indeed, "The Deluge" does depict a dark scene—literally a dark scene—so dark that from a distance it appears to be almost entirely a black canvas. Quite what was in the mind of Jacob More when he created this painting we will never know, but authentic art never restricts the observer to the intention of the artist. Closer scrutiny of "The Deluge" offers the possibility of an interpretation which connects the dark visual aspect not with dread and the enormity of the idea of the end of the world, but rather with something less awesome and more expectant. The physical darkness of deep greens and greys actually harbours great hope. The exquisitely painted sunlight is so central and captivating that it draws our attention away from the intimate scene of salvation and human resilience which is taking place in the half-light of early morning or evening. It is as if the tradition of the sublime which equates magnificent destruction and catastrophe with darkness is subverted here, for this is actually a picture of life, of survival, of a small remnant preparing to start again. The light is appearing over the horizon but the re-birth is happening under the canvas of night. This grand and, on the face of it, solemn work has, for me, come to epitomize the way in which darkness is assumed to be inherently fearful. The viewer, looking at the painting and seeing darkness, might subconsciously expect to understand that what is depicted is representative of something adverse. Yet, if the Sublime dark-negative association can be overcome, a wholly different perception is rendered possible and pleasure emerges, not from the evocation of fear and terror, but rather from a sense of life, human determination, and future possibility. Darkness can evoke these things if only we can free ourselves from the shackles of association.

III

In Chapter 6 I will consider how darkness is used in a much more positive way within the art world, but the negative association espoused within the movement of the Sublime is one which holds fast to this day. It has influenced many contemporary artists, particularly those working in popular culture, to represent music and film which has an apocalyptic emphasis. The graphic illustrations for many so-called "disaster movies" or computer games owe much to the tradition of the Sublime, in particular to the artist John Martin, whose works include dark depictions of scenes connected in the imagination to Milton's *Paradise Lost*. Typical of the genre would be the image used to publicize the 2009 film *2012*, which portrays huge swathes of a brooding and shadowy Manhattan being uprooted and flooded by a mega-tsunami.[52] Also typical is the computer action game "Hellgate: London",[53] depicting gaping craters opening up the streets of London under deeply dark and foreboding skies. The resonances with Martin's work are strong, and the graphics associated with the musical traditions of Heavy Metal are an important aspect of his legacy. Black and Death Metal and Goth Rock, in particular, are frequently illustrated by dark and menacing graphics of mythical figures and earthly destruction, reflecting extreme themes of violence and death within the lyrics. A number of bands have used John Martin's paintings as album covers, and this quotation which I picked up on a website whilst researching the theme cannot possibly go without reproduction here:

Martin is so Metal that he makes the musical genre redundant.[54]

The connection is so evident that it was the subject of an event at the Laing Art Gallery in Newcastle upon Tyne in 2006, "1,000 Days in Sodom: Metal Music and the Paintings of John Martin". The lyrics which follow emphasize the enduring association between the darkness of much sublime art and the content of songs recorded on albums represented by such art. The painting formerly attributed to John Martin, "The Fallen Angels Entering Pandemonium", is used as the cover of the 1980 album *Angel Witch* by the British Heavy Metal band of the same name. The album explores themes of destruction, fear and apocalypse.

Similarly, Martin's painting "Christ Stilleth the Tempest" is the cover for the 2012 album *Vast Oceans Lachrymose* by Doom Metal band (not my description!) While Heaven Wept. These lyrics are from the track "To Wander the Void":

> A million miles from everything the emptiness is everywhere
> the lone and level sands stretch as far as I can see
> nothing but the hollowed eyes of skulls
>   and ancient bones despair
> remains of those who wandered this wasteland vast before me[55]

The attempt by artists, as with theologians, to express those things which go beyond human comprehension or experience is perhaps instinctive, fired by the desire for creativity and understanding and a capacity for deep imagination. It has led to some of the most magnificent works of art and music known to humankind. Yet the reliance in some spheres upon a negative visual metaphor of darkness has served to perpetuate an idea which is at best misleading and at worst debilitating as the boundary between the real and the imaginary becomes blurred, and darkness is afforded a fearful identity that it does not deserve, and need not own. When we talk of being afraid of the dark, what is it we actually mean? Is it the darkness itself of which we are afraid, or the associated conditions of isolation, danger, death, claustrophobia, and—in parts of the world—bitter cold?

It seems to me that we are less likely to express a sense of fear if we are standing in the dark in a safe, open space, in familiar surroundings with a group of friends. However, if the dark space is limited, enclosed, or unfamiliar, infused with an element of danger, or if we find ourselves in that situation alone, then suddenly the situation becomes more fearful, and it is likely to be the darkness which is articulated as the source of that fear rather than any of the other factors. Find yourself in a small cave, underground, on your own, yet in a bright light, and you might still be likely to say you are afraid. Light does not necessarily remove fear, and may even be a source of it, depending on what else is in the cave that is best left hidden from view!

To go down a slightly different yet related track, it would not be usual to associate the occurrence of bad things with it being light. Yet bad things happen in the light; even broad daylight is not an indicator of immunity from incident or attack. On the other hand, it is a commonly articulated contention that bad things happen in the dark: which, as within the light, they of course do! But did darkness in itself ever hurt anyone? Has darkness ever pulled out a rifle and shot anyone or abducted a child or stolen a wallet? There are questions of cause and effect at play here which seem to have conspired against darkness, making her the scapegoat for our fears and discomforts and a culprit "de rigueur". The origins of the association may well lie deep within the human psyche and deep in the past, but I do not believe they lie within our soul.

IV

In the inner-city church in which I work, the pattern of our communal life is to some extent dictated by the seasons. In the spring and summer even the most elderly and infirm members of the church are happy to be out and about, attending choir practice, even church meetings if they have nothing better to do! Yet with the onset of autumn, so much grinds to a halt as the mantra of "We can't go out after dark" begins to resonate. The fear is palpable, and among the more mature folk all but a few hardy and sprightly souls retreat into the artificial light of their homes as soon as the sun sets. Yet it never, in reality, gets dark. Except perhaps for those with visual impairments of one kind or another, the streets of Stoke Newington feel pretty much the same in the evening as they do in the morning. All is visible, the buses are still running, so I wonder what the real root cause of the fear is. Even if the statistics do not back it up, the association of darkness with crime, cold, and danger holds sway.

In his book *Nocturne: A Journey in Search of Moonlight*,[56] James Attlee reflects upon a move made by some local councils in recent years to turn off street lighting for a few hours in the middle of the night as a green and money-saving measure. The locals are up in arms and the local press are happy to collude with the idea that the reduced lighting measure will take the areas concerned back into the so-called Dark Ages. Interviews with police concerned about the possible increase in crime and with motoring organizations about implications for road safety are quoted with indignation, alongside photographs showing the apparent pitch-blackness into which the streets are plunged after the lights are turned off. Attlee, however, points out that the photographs show that the lack of lighting does not equate with pitch-blackness and that "anyone stepping beyond the halogen glare of their porch security lighting and letting their eyes adjust for a minute or so would have no problem navigating the neighbourhood."[57] The main fear expressed through the newspaper article is one of increased crime, although as the author points out, this particular neighbourhood is in a fairly affluent area and has a low rate of crime. He goes on to say:

> The genius of the author of this article is to combine this deep-seated fear of crime with our primal fear of darkness. Even where there isn't any crime, people lie awake at night worrying about it. And even when there isn't really any darkness, to the intimidated and the elderly, who spend long periods shut in their houses being told by people on their televisions it is dangerous to go outside, it appears pitch black. Why does it seem so dark? *Because they have so many lights on!* Meanwhile the message of the night sky, an illuminated manuscript a dweller in the Dark Ages could read as easily as his descendants read a newspaper, is erased by a generation too frightened to go to sleep without leaving a lamp burning beside them.[58]

In my younger days, before I could drive and when I was reliant upon others to do so, it was usual to expect to complete any journey before it got dark. I remember my grandparents saying it, and my own parents: "We need to leave now or we won't be home before it's dark!" I didn't question it at the time, although I have questioned it since, and apart from those times when it offers a welcome excuse to make an early departure from a tense or uninviting situation, it's not a practice I have absorbed into my own repertoire of driving habits. Nevertheless, like venturing out as a pedestrian, taking to the road *en voiture* after dark carries with it, for many people, a sense of fear and dread, in spite of sophisticated automobile headlight systems, and well-lit roads. Looking at the statistics on a superficial level, this fear is not entirely unfounded; there is a higher proportion of fatal car accidents at night. In the UK, twenty-five per cent of journeys by car are undertaken at night, whilst forty per cent of all serious accidents happen between the hours of 7 p.m. and 8 a.m.[59] However, in order to do justice to those figures, it is necessary to understand some of the reasons behind them. It is too easy simply to conclude that darkness is the direct cause—especially when we learn that older drivers have fewer accidents at night and that disproportionate numbers of young drivers, especially young men, are injured at night. The AA Motoring Trust's 2005 scoping study on the subject of night-time accidents drew attention to the mitigating factors which were often behind them. Factors such as glare caused by oncoming traffic and poor road markings, plus young drivers pushing their driving skills to the limit on rural roads and carrying too many passengers, are all factors associated with night-time driving which heighten the risk of accidents. It also seems intuitive that there are more likely to be drunk drivers on the roads at night. So until headlights can be more effectively adjusted, until there is better discipline in dipping lights for oncoming vehicles, until roads are more widely maintained to a high standard, and until people, young and old, take responsibility for their own driving practices, it is likely that darkness will still get the blame.

V

I first heard about Dans le Noir?—a restaurant in Clerkenwell, an area of London close to Kings Cross station—from a friend of mine who had read a review in a Sunday newspaper on 1 April. She told me that in Dans le Noir? (literally "In the Dark?" or "In the Black?") guests eat in a pitch-black dining room and are served by blind and partially-sighted waiters. As we discussed this apparently ludicrous, yet strangely intriguing and appealing concept, we quickly came to the conclusion that it must have been an April Fool's joke: such is the tendency of the British broadsheets on the first day of the fourth month to offer stories which, whilst being humorous and frivolous, contain within them just the right amount of plausibility to test the insight of the most hardened sceptic. Nevertheless, no subsequent admission of jocundity appeared, and Alison's curiosity was such that she drove past the address offered in the newspaper review in order to corroborate the existence of the said restaurant. And corroborate its existence she did. In fact, far from being a joke, so popular is Dans le Noir? and its enlightened darkness that it has become a global chain with partner establishments in Barcelona, St Petersburg, Kiev, Paris, and New York. At the time, the restaurant website said that what the restaurant offers is a "perceptual awakening", the idea being that one's sense of taste is heightened by the removal of the sense of sight. The newspaper reviewer had offered two options of grading for ambience—either one star or five stars—depending, he said, on your point of view. At the time I felt sure I would give it five, always rating ambience on a par with, if not higher than, the quality of food in a restaurant, always seeking dimly lit shadiness rather than crisp white table cloths and walls. The reviewer, however, didn't like it at all. "If you're serious about food," he wrote, "go somewhere where they leave the lights on." So, of course, being serious about both food and darkness, I had to find out for myself.

It seemed right to go with some of the people I love and trust most—not only because I could rely on their honesty in terms of reflecting on the experience, mitigating my tendency to eulogize darkness and to drift into mawkish sentimentality, but also to test out the idea that dependable and convivial company makes darkness less threatening. If, as the publicity claims, the experience demands a "transfer of trust"[60] between client and staff, then I wanted to be with people among whom I felt safe! My party were all aware of my interest and my intention to write a book about the positive nature of darkness. So I wasn't quite prepared for the palpable apprehension and uncertainty as we gathered in a nearby pub just around the corner from Dans le Noir? a couple of hours prior to our booking. It is possible that I diminish the significance of the degree of fear which darkness evokes in some people, so strong is my conviction that it is a state of pure beauty, yet I could not ignore it here. We were led to our table through heavy black velvet curtains, leaving the dim but deliberately lit waiting room, and guided by a blind waiter who led us in single file, hand to shoulder, one behind the other. The dining room was utterly dark, pitch-black, and I was immediately reminded of the ice cave in Svalbard, the only other place in my consciousness at that time which could match such a level of impenetrable darkness. I could feel the unease of my daughter, albeit seated as she was between two beloved friends and in touch with me diagonally across the table. Another party were seated adjacent to us and within seconds one of their number had made her excuses and left, unable to cope with the environment. Whatever the reasons, darkness truly has the capacity to instil terror and panic. Yet as we realized that the lack of light did not prevent us from recognizing one another's voices, and that we could function, pouring wine and water without spillage and passing bread one to the other, something sacramental and sensual emerged which drew us together in a way different from any other, ordinary dinner gathering.

Stripped of body language and facial expression, we were forced to listen more closely. Having only the sense of hearing to rely on, we were unable to indicate the intended direction of a comment by using our line of sight, so it was harder to have more than one conversation taking place around the table simultaneously. We worked this out eventually and found a pattern of allowing one person to speak at a time in a way which engaged everyone at the table. Those known among us for being conversationalists and professional talkers were strangely silent. Knowing that we could not be seen allowed us each in our own way to countenance the relaxation of the normal guards of social convention; we did not have to worry if a hair was out of place, or if lipstick was smudged, or a blob of something unmentionable was on display in an inappropriate place. With eyes closed, elbows on the table, and unseen intimate touches, and with who knows what else the infra-red security camera operator saw (we did not dare to think of that person as being present at our table), we fumbled our way through our meal. We did not know the exact nature of the dishes in front of us—each choosing from a general menu of meat, fish, or vegetarian—but using our noses and our fingers and thumbs, as well as knives and forks, we pondered and tasted our food in a way which would never normally happen. One of my friends said that she felt the need to give a running commentary on what she was eating, so that we could share her experience as she gradually discovered what was on her plate.

Another friend reflected subsequently:

> From the first moment of our slow crocodile approach to our table, to the reverse walk back an hour and a half later, we knew what it felt like to have to rely on other senses to inform and protect us. Hearing, touch, smell, and taste became more pronounced, sharper, more dependable.

He didn't like the darkness, he said he felt controlled by it, and in listening to how it made him feel I began to understand more fully the concept of "transferring trust".

In order to survive darkness we need to transfer trust from one familiar sense to another (or at least to use senses for different purposes from those which are usual). We need to transfer trust from self to other, particularly to others who can support and guide us. We need to transfer trust from that of total understanding to that of partial understanding (we all wanted to know whether any attention had been given to the décor of the restaurant!). We need to transfer trust from being in control to being, to some extent, out of control. Darkness has the capacity to evoke distress, more than many other conditions, because of the demands it can make on us to step outside our personal comfort zone. Only if we are able to begin to make that crucial transfer of trust can we begin to experience darkness without a sense of discomfort or fear.

In his 1921 novel *The Path of the King*, in which he explores the nature of greatness, John Buchan tells a delightful story of a child's determination to transfer trust—not that the young boy would have expressed it that way! Biorn, who is the ancestor of an auspicious line of leaders, stretching all the way to Abraham Lincoln, invents a bedtime game playing with the darkness in his room, and so begins a journey shaped by vulnerability, bravery, and stoicism:

> When Biorn was a very little boy in his father's stead at Hightown he had a play of his own making for the long winter nights. At the back end of the hall, where the men sat at ale, was a chamber

which the thralls used of a morning—a place which smelt of hams and meal and good provender. There a bed had been made for him when he forsook his cot in the women's quarters. When the door was shut it was black dark, save for a thin crack of light from the wood fire and torches of the hall. The crack made on the earthen floor a line like a golden river. Biorn, cuddled up on a bench in his little bear-skin, was drawn like a moth to that stream of light. With his heart beating fast he would creep to it and stand for a moment with his small body bathed in the radiance. The game was not to come back at once, but to foray into the farther darkness before returning to the sanctuary of bed. That took all the fortitude in Biorn's heart, and not till the thing was dared and done could he go happily to sleep.

One night Leif the Outborn watched him at his game. Sometimes the man was permitted to sleep there when he had been making sport for the housecarles.

"Behold an image of life!" he had said in his queer outland speech. "We pass from darkness to darkness with but an instant of light between. You are born for high deeds, princeling. Many would venture from the dark to the light, but it takes a stout breast to voyage into the farther dark."[61]

Perhaps in these things—in the charming tale of Biorn's night-time game and in the expedition to Dans le Noir?—I am beginning to get closer to the heart of the association between fear and darkness. Some recognition of inevitability also emerges in the quest to understand the use of darkness as a metaphor for what is surely the ultimate transfer of trust—that from life to death.

That there is an association between fear and darkness is incontrovertible. Yet the roots of the association are not necessarily to be found in some innately terrifying characteristic of darkness. Rather, it is possible that fears arise as a result of the demands and challenges which darkness places upon us. Some of these demands can be overcome with practical solutions, some require us to delve a little deeper into our human nature, but it is an undertaking worthy of attention. For in the darkness are deeper riches to be found as we are compelled to transfer trust, to move closer, to look more deeply, and to explore the fullest range of our senses. Which one of us has not, at some time or another, deliberately closed our eyes whilst listening to a piece of music or a song, in order to appreciate more fully the quality of the sound and to allow our heart and mind to focus on the melody and lyrics, unimpeded by visual distractions? Darkness can be sublime, but not necessarily through the evocation of fear or danger, rather as an indicator of a seductive and aesthetically pleasing environment which has the capacity to stimulate awe and wonder and to lift us beyond ourselves, into a state of pleasure and calm.

Svalbard Journey
First Visit, 8 January 2013

Arriving in Svalbard, I find the daytime darkness is darker than I ever imagined it would be, the disorientation acute. I am conscious of an extreme landscape surrounding me, mountainous shapes that suddenly appear out of nowhere as the eye adjusts to the light level. My instinctive reaction is that it will be good to see the backdrop to the town of Longyearbyen more clearly in the morning. And then the realization strikes: the morning light will be just like the afternoon light, and just like the evening and the night-time light. And with that comes the understanding that in my time here I will need to learn to see things differently. I realize for the first time an obvious fact—that when it is dark it is harder to see the detail in the wider picture. So, in forgoing the detail, can I find a different "seeing" in an appreciation of the shapes and basic forms and the patterns they create against the deep blue of the sky and in relationship to the lights of the town? In the daylight do we see the details at the expense of these more nebulous features?

I want to see details in the dark, I will of course have to move closer in.

CHAPTER 5

The Nurturing Darkness

Almost we feel a longing for the darkness, for the deep unknowing
obscurity with its shining dreams and its waiting for the return
of life.

Christiane Ritter[62]

I

It happened very suddenly, although on reflection it had been coming a
long time; one day, my friend was apparently committed and alive, the
sound and soul of the party, the energy of the group—his laughter, skilled
innuendo, drive, and loyalty a familiar source of comfort and security
to those who loved him. Then he simply stopped. Unable to move, eat,
or breathe without the deliberate persistence of others. The reason?
A "breakdown"—the causes of which we all knew at least something.
"Depression"—probably a medically more accurate definition but not
one easily assigned to this skilled actor, whose masks we had all chosen
to collude with. When I went to see him, on that first day, in the early
summer mid-afternoon, the darkness seemed to have been carefully crafted:
a firmly shut door, a very low, dim light, closed curtains, a dressing gown
hood pulled up over his head and down over his brow. He was barely
able to speak, although he was able to say, "It's dark in here." Another
visiting friend offered to open the curtains. "No," replied my friend, "in
here", as he placed his curled fist over his heart and tapped it lightly. He
stayed in the darkness for many days. We knew things were beginning
to change when the curtains opened and the hood was withdrawn, and

gradually a recognized and loved person emerged, having taken the first tentative steps on the long road to recovery. In articulating a sense of inner darkness my friend was simply falling upon a tried and tested metaphor—one which we all use in our clumsy and human attempts to convey all those complicated, negative emotions connected with the things which cause real fear—loss, isolation, betrayal, poverty, pain, a sense of failure. But in those days of utter withdrawal, it seemed to me as if the external darkness was necessary, critical even; the whisperer of relief, the facilitator of a healing period of hibernation, allowing the world and its terrors and threats to be held at bay whilst inner resources reconnected and recharged.

As a young student I had on my study bedroom wall the classic text of disputed authorship, "Footprints in the Sand". Sadly, the words are over-used now—a profound and poetic statement of God's unconditional companionship relegated to cheesily illustrated and hastily laminated posters sold in New Age and a certain genre of Christian bookshops. I realize now in retrospect that, to my shame, I didn't understand it fully at the time. I thought the image of the single set of footprints in the sand was mine and that the pinnacle of revelation, "It was then that I carried you", was simply a statement of the fact that when I felt abandoned, alone, or sad, God would help me. This is, of course, a perfectly valid exegesis, but it rather misses the more profound point which I can now see the writer was making, which is that the single set of footprints was actually intended to be God's, who was, at that point of my spiritual or material deprivation, physically—actually—carrying me.

When considering the meaning of darkness, it seems to be very easy to fall into the same trap as I did with "Footprints". It is usual to speak of God helping and caring for people during the "dark" times of life: in other words, during times which are hard in some way. I often hear people saying something to the effect of, "It was a very dark period of my life but I knew God was with me." This is a tried and tested way of speaking about suffering, and understanding God's role within it; there is a familiarity and assurance in the idea that God accompanies us *through* our metaphorical darknesses. But is it also possible to see God *as the darkness itself*? A darkness which carries us to safety, a place of hibernation in which to hide or regenerate? In this way of thinking, God offers us physical darkness as a gift. In the shadow and lightlessness, in the need to close our eyes and hide ourselves away in sleep and tearfulness, God's shade is the space needed to recuperate, to revive, simply to "be". In times of stress and loss, darkness ceases to be a metaphor for humanity's pain, but rather becomes the pathway through to the other side of it. In the guise of darkness itself, God offers support, companionship, and presence, and the stillness and time we need to recover.

II

In 1794 the German Romantic poet Friedrich von Hardenberg (later known as Novalis) met and fell in love with Sophie von Kühn (we shall not allow contemporary sensibilities and moralities to get in the way here—she was only thirteen years of age when they were engaged to be married, while he was twenty-three!). Tragically, Sophie died of tuberculosis at the age of fifteen, before they could be married. Novalis was reportedly heartbroken and in the years after Sophie's death, as a way of making sense of it and of dealing with his grief, he wrote his *Hymnen an die Nacht* (*Hymns to the Night*). In six prose poems interspersed with verse, Novalis uses the night as a potent metaphor for death—but not, as might be expected, as a bleak and morbid reflection upon the fearful and devastating nature of life's end. Rather, for Novalis, night becomes the point of transition from life to death, a mystical moment within which we come into the presence, not only of God, but also of the one whom we have loved and lost, and even of eternity itself:

> Once when I was shedding bitter tears, when, dissolved in pain, my hope was melting away, and I stood alone by the barren mound which in its narrow dark bosom hid the vanished form of my Life, lonely as never yet was lonely man, driven by anxiety unspeakable, powerless, and no longer anything but a conscious misery; as there I looked about me for help, unable to go on or to turn back, and clung to the fleeting, extinguished life with an

endless longing: then, out of the blue distances—from the hills of my ancient bliss, came a shiver of twilight—and at once snapt the bond of birth, the chains of the Light. Away fled the glory of the world, and with it my mourning; the sadness flowed together into a new, unfathomable world. Thou, soul of the Night, heavenly Slumber, didst come upon me; the region gently upheaved itself; over it hovered my unbound, newborn spirit.[63]

I must remember to tell my family to read Novalis at my funeral instead of the twenty-third psalm! Don't misunderstand me, it's not that I don't appreciate its message of God's graceful and life-giving provision in the face of testing situations, a message which has resonated with generations of dying and grieving people. It is not without good reason that it is the most commonly read piece of scripture in Christian funeral services:

> The LORD is my shepherd, I shall not want.
>> He makes me lie down in green pastures;
> he leads me beside still waters;
>> he restores my soul.
> He leads me in right paths
>> for his name's sake.
> Even though I walk through the darkest valley,
>> I fear no evil;
> for you are with me;
>> your rod and your staff —
>> they comfort me.
> You prepare a table before me
>> in the presence of my enemies;
> you anoint my head with oil;
>> my cup overflows.
> Surely goodness and mercy shall follow me
>> all the days of my life,
> and I shall dwell in the house of the LORD
>> my whole life long.[64]

Psalm 23

However, glorious poetry that it is, Psalm 23 must bear some responsibility for the way in which ideas of death, darkness, and despair have become conflated in the English language. The heart of the psalm, verse 4, can reasonably be translated as either, "Even though I walk through the valley of the shadow of death, I will fear no evil;"[65] or, as it is printed above, "Even though I walk through the darkest valley, I fear no evil."[66] The origin is a rare compound phrase in Hebrew, צלמות, *tsalmavet* (*tsal* or "shadow" and *mavet* or "death"), which is translated in the New International Version of the Bible as "shadow of death" but is translated elsewhere in Scripture simply as "darkness". The roots of the phrase encompass the ideas of both "shadow" and "death" and are suggestive of despair or danger, represented by the metaphor of impenetrable darkness. Interestingly, I am aware of many accounts of people going through so-called "near-death experiences" who have described the pull towards, not darkness, but rather a bright light. However, the association of death with the idea of a dark and fearful final state—even though God is with us in it—is well cemented within the popular human consciousness. In William Shakespeare's play *Measure for Measure* (Act III, Scene 1), Claudio, in preparing for his execution, says:

> If I must die,
> I will encounter darkness as a bride,
> and hug it in mine arms.

Nevertheless, this was not always the case. Whilst humankind has continuously struggled to understand what happens at the point of dying, the most ancient mythology offers a narrative which is not characterized by the association of death and darkness with dread and evil. Ancient peoples watched the cycle of the moon and quite naturally made associations between its regular disappearance and re-appearance and the death and rebirth of the body. Myths, philosophies, and theologies developed from the heart of this Neolithic reflection, and the presence of a sacred, hidden underworld—a place of both death and new life—underpinned them all.

This era heralded the advent of agriculture. The new agrarian communities acknowledged a powerful force at work in the darkness of the earth, as they observed the transformation of a sown seed, dying in the earth so that it might ultimately become the source of life-giving nourishment.

Early European and North American myths of creation described the seeds of humanity incubating in the underworld, germinating and pushing up through the surface, sprouting like seeds to be gathered when in full bloom, or emerging up through the soil as fully formed people.[67] The earth was a womb, giving birth—like a woman—to fruit which had been created by the planting of a seed inside her. Underground labyrinths from this period suggest that pilgrims sought to journey to what they believed to be the source of their being, their place of origin, entering into the womb of the Earth which was their Mother Goddess. This Mother Goddess took on various culturally specific manifestations—Asherah or Anat in Syria, Isis in Egypt, Demeter or Aphrodite in Greece—yet she was always a goddess who not only brought life but who also wrought destruction, reflecting the harsh and dangerous reality of the agricultural existence as experienced by its practitioners. While the emerging mythology always pointed towards the restoration of a balanced and harmonious state of affairs, the destruction and ruin at its core was never totally conquered. These were myths grounded in the reality of day-to-day life and death, focused around a pantheon of gods and goddesses who reflected the battles and struggles of the people. Gods were gruesomely destroyed in battles of blood-curdling proportions, their remains strewn on the ground like scattered seed, before they reappeared, brought back to life like the wheat that springs up green. In other myths, gods were forced into the underworld as punishment, or made the journey willingly for other reasons; whatever the storyline, their presence in the depths of the Earth became the life force for the harvest. At the heart of these complex and varied myths is a consistency of meaning—life and death are inseparable, there cannot be one without the other.

In Neolithic times, of course, death was a harsh but commonplace reality of life. Farmers were at the mercy of nature—often an unreliable, fickle, and violent partner—and with each pregnancy women faced the very real prospect of death in childbirth. Life and death intermingled with an intensity unknown in the modern Western world. They were opposite sides of the same coin, and the dark underworld became the stage for the playing out of their mutual dependency. It was not symbolic of evil, rather understood as the place where death preceded birth, and the creation of new life. The website for Historic Scotland describes the

Neolithic tomb at Maeshowe on the Scottish islands of Orkney as one of Europe's finest chambered tombs.[68] Five thousand years ago the community enshrined their theology of human mortality within an extraordinary feat of architecture. A low and gradually descending passage leading into the tomb has been positioned such that around the time of the winter solstice, the shortest day of the year, a sharp ray of sunlight pierces the tomb at sunset and settles upon the back wall of the chamber. From within the darkness new life emerges.

In the Roman world, the god of the underworld, Dis Pater, was worshipped as a god of fertility, plenty, and prosperity. His location in the underworld was a direct result of the fact that the Greco-Roman Empire was considered to be the repository for the mineral wealth—precious gems and metals—of the whole earth. In spite of his position in the darkness of the underworld, Dis Pater was not a sinister character but rather one who affirmed the underworld as the source of life and abundance.

The resurrection of Christ from within the sealed darkness of the garden tomb in which his body was laid is resonant of, and consistent with, these ancient convictions. From the devastation and destruction of the crucifixion, Christ emerges as an eternal, spiritual entity, whose influence continues in the lives of those who, through their baptism and commitment to a particular way of living, choose to follow him. The God who dies violently comes back to life again to restore balance and harmony in the world.

It was only much later that Dis Pater was conflated with the Greek god Hades, a name which along with the Hebrew *sheol* (שאול) means "grave" and has come to be understood as the place of the dead. Hades was not considered to be evil, however, and although he was the stern and fearful ruler of the underworld and associated with death, mythology portrays him as one who was just and concerned with maintaining order and balance. Yet in the Christian tradition, up to and including the present day, Hades is one of the terms which has become synonymous with Hell, largely due to the reference in Luke's Gospel to it being a place of agony and torment (Luke 16:23).

From the sixteenth century onwards there was a move in the West away from the fragile and perilous agriculturally based societies as industrialization took hold. With the Enlightenment and Scientific

Revolution there was a demise in the potency of myth as the primary tool for explaining the way the world works. As the monotheistic religions embraced the re-emerging philosophical rationality, the fate of darkness was sealed as it became equated with death and evil, just as light was associated with goodness and life. Today it is true to say that there is a deep suspicion of myth within the Christian tradition. The inability (or unwillingness) to distinguish between what is truthful and what is factual is common; consequently, many branches of Christian theology cannot see beyond the heaven and hell dichotomy. What is more, light and dark remain separated, used as distinctive metaphors reflecting a dualistic framework that has no roots in those older Christian and pre-Christian understandings which embraced the cyclical nature of the universe, drew no distinction between life and death, and hesitated to associate darkness with evil and light with good.

So it is perhaps not so surprising that in spite of the clear and hopeful articulation of the continuation of life beyond death which is held at the heart of the Christian faith, fear of death is still so commonplace. The concepts of darkness, death, fear, and evil have become muddled in a melting pot of metaphor which leaves the supposed ultimate glory of the Christian religion hard to access and comprehend. Death is scary—the fact that there is the assurance of something wonderful beyond it is immaterial. By and large, we do not want to die. And that is not just about the fact that we might, if we are lucky, be enjoying this life and do not want to leave those who love us in a state of mourning. It is because the valley of death is dark and we have learned to fear the dark.

Svalbard Journey
Third Visit, All Saints' Day 1 November 2015

It is All Saints' Day and it is the tradition of the community of Svalbardkirke to hold a simple ceremony in the small graveyard on the hillside along the road from the church.

It is a misty day. The clouds are heavy and for the first time here I experience rain: a thick ice rain, neither snow nor hail, definitely rain, but almost syrupy in substance, it lends an air of melancholy to the ceremony. Gathering outside the church after the gentle morning service we are offered candles to carry with us—giant versions of the small hand-held votives with cardboard shields that I am familiar with using on Christmas Eve. It is only after some time, after the chaos and laughter of their lighting one from the other, that we slowly and cautiously begin our walk. Someone falls hard on the treacherously icy path, and I am reminded of the text we had heard just a short while previously from Matthew's Gospel about being the salt of the earth (Matthew 5:13). If salt has lost its saltiness, the Gospel tells us, it is no longer good for anything and is thrown out to be trampled on. But, I find myself thinking, in that trampling someone's life could have been saved! Thankfully my fallen companion is OK, but had there been more grit on the path she would not have fallen at all. That useless salt! How easily we discard and define things as being of little worth, without attempting to uncover the potential treasure within. Salt and darkness, together facing the disrespect of a judgemental world!

The darkness surrounds the solemn and reverential tone of our procession. It reflects our mood and offers a sense of accompanying as we make our way towards the cemetery. It is about 12.30 p.m. This is the time of the half-light when the sun never quite rises but is able to shed some feeble rays above the horizon for a few hours. It is a bright darkness, characteristic of these days just prior to the onset of the deep Polar Night. As we walk, I sense that each one of us is holding the memory of a loved one, or a known one, their lives reflected in the burning torches and cradled in the twilight. We arrive at the tiny cemetery with its few rows of plain white crosses, each with a black plaque at the centre bearing the identity of the deceased. Today the rain has melted much of the snow upon the steep mountainsides which form the dramatic backdrop to the burial ground, so the crosses are oddly camouflaged against this canvas of black rock streaked with icy white residue.

The ceremony begins with the sound of a lone trumpet playing the tune of the hymn, "Abide with me". The sound echoes back from the rock face and the words come into my mind: "Abide with me; fast falls the eventide; the darkness deepens; Lord, with me abide!" Surely the Lord is abiding with us in this moment, as the darkness literally deepens around us. We remember and commemorate those who have died and give thanks for their lives and their abiding memories. I try to imagine the remains of the bodies being held in the darkness of the earth below, and the souls, released from them, being nurtured by God in another-worldly, mysterious realm of darkness and light. A visiting choir sings a Celtic blessing: "May the road rise up to meet you . . . may God hold you in the embrace of his palm until we meet again." A member of the choir can barely conceal a sorrow which the ceremony awakens in her. I later discover that a member of the choir had died just two days previously and that they will sing this same song at his funeral in a few days' time. A comforting arm is placed around her as she tries to restrain her sobbing. She does not need to restrain it, of course, because in this place and in this moment there is a solidarity of grief, and the roots of the grief go deep into the shared ground upon which we all stand. This is the ultimate paradox of the Christian faith—that love leads to grief, yet grief leads to hope; that while we can feel such intense sadness we can, at the same time, be instilled with confidence that the one who has been lost to us lives again. Sometimes we try too hard to understand this; to add it to our box of formulae about the way God works. That is perhaps why we try and hold back the tears. Our rational selves find it hard to live with the mystery of the darkness and light being both alike to God. As I make my way back down the hill, the tops of the mountains merge with and disappear into the clouds, and as I continue to reflect upon the never-ending cycle of life and death, of beginnings and ends, of darkness and light, of balance and of hope, I realise that it is impossible to tell where the snow ends and the clouds begin.

III

In the world of alternative therapies—at least, those available to Western middle classes seeking relief from the stresses of the modern world—floatation therapy is an emerging star. Shortly after my first return from Svalbard, and in my continued pursuit of darkness, it seemed only right that I should avail myself of the special offer which appeared in my inbox for a one-hour session at a clinic offering such an experience.

I knew that floatation therapy involved being isolated in total darkness in an enclosed chamber, floating in a shallow solution of Epsom salts and water heated to body temperature. I knew about its supposed healing and calming effects. I knew that it had evolved into a form of therapy from research carried out in the 1950s into the physiological and psychological impacts of sensory deprivation. I did not know, however, that its modern manifestation, in comfortable, sterile, fashionable spas and salons, is just the tip of the iceberg when it comes to the deliberate use of darkness as a state within which physical, mental, and spiritual well-being can be achieved. It was only after my own immersion that I wanted to know more and stumbled upon the mysterious world of the Tibetan Dark Retreat. For thousands of years, Tibetan monks have entered into seclusion, silence, and darkness for periods of up to seven weeks. In this isolated space they make a journey of self-discovery, growing spiritually and—so they believe—preparing for their entry into the next world.

Many of the physiological and psychological benefits of darkness have been touched on elsewhere in this book—a rest for our eyes and an enhancement of the other senses, alterations in body chemistry, a slower and simpler pace of life, and so on. The Dark Retreat offers all these things, of course, but it also emphasizes the internal and spiritual, the opportunity to explore the true inner nature of the self whilst freed from external stimulation, leading to an improved quality of life overall. In his poem "Radiant Heart of Darkness" Martin Lowenthal, a Western practitioner of the Dark Retreat, describes something of its practice and purpose:

In this dark space
thoughts, feelings, and plans
have boundless room
and no place.

So I gaze into blank blackness
praising memories of light and sky
and settle into
this unknown darkness.

With gratitude for the pulsing in palms
and cool breeze of inhaling breath,
I sit poised on the edge of tears, bliss
and I know not what.

Looking into endless, embracing dark,
in this still moment

are these bright lights and inaudible sounds
plays of fancy
or the true nature
of a freshly opened heart?[69]

As is the case with many forms of Eastern spiritual practice, the Dark Retreat has found its way into the West. The intensity and length of the traditional Tibetan Dark Retreat makes it prohibitive for many (if not most) people who might otherwise want to experience the benefits of the practice. However, thanks to Western practitioners such as Martin Lowenthal, it is now possible to enter into shorter dark retreats of just a few days. The solitary immersion in total darkness remains central, but the principles are distilled in such a way as to make them accessible and meaningful to people who are doing everyday jobs and holding down a regular family and social life. As Lowenthal describes it:

> The purpose of such retreats is to relax into the nature of our own being, allowing the mind to discover its natural awareness. In

this relaxation we discover the essential qualities of the authentic presence, inner lights and visions, the energies of aliveness, silence, and listening, and sacred wisdom. In time we adopt an open heart posture of praise, gratitude, love, compassion, and peace. To find that relaxation and experience that wisdom means confronting and transcending our core fears, unspoken longings, and patterns of denial and addiction.

In a dark retreat, the play of bodymind is exposed more clearly, without the presence of the usual multitude of external stimuli. External darkness becomes a screen for the performance of the internal theater of images, stories, and reactions.[70]

In other contexts, the retreat has been enculturated for primarily therapeutic purposes. In the Czech Republic, Andrew Urbiš, a psychologist and holistic therapist, offers "darkness therapy" in a specially adapted residence called "Vila Mátma", which can be translated as "the house which is a tomb", or perhaps more palatably, "my darkness"! Dr Urbiš claims that recovery periods following surgery and for conditions such as eczema can be halved with the use of darkness therapy. These claims were born out by Czech reporter Sylvie Dymáková.[71] In 2014, showing clear signs of stress and lacking in energy, she entered Vila Mátma for seven days. At first she experienced anxiety, fear, and a sense of crisis in which she believed someone was in the room with her. Realistic dreams and visualizations followed. Only then, after about three days alone in the dark with only her thoughts for company, did the regeneration begin and the creativity surface, and she emerged from the darkness emotionally charged and revived.

I have yet to experience first-hand the depth of an authentic dark retreat, although it already features high up my bucket list! But my brief experience of the floatation tank has offered a glimpse into both the riches and the challenges that will be in store. Inevitably, the mysterious power of floatation therapy has been subjected to scientific research, much of which testifies to the discernible and beneficial effects of entering into total darkness for significant periods of time. When I entered the clinic in which I was to experience floatation therapy, the reception area had been carefully crafted to offer a gradual introduction to the removal of light. The environment offered low lighting and the paintings on the wall were dark, some of them predominantly black. I immediately felt my shoulders drop and my breath begin to slow. I entered the floatation chamber naked—even the sense of fabric against the skin can create points of pressure which detract from the overall experience of sensory deprivation. I was reassured by the location of an emergency release button within easy reach, although I had no doubt that I would not need it! Surprised by the shallow depth of the strong saline water—just a few inches needed to support my body without it touching the bottom—I lay down and the chamber was sealed, plunging me into total darkness the likeness of which I had only ever experienced before in the depths of the ice cave in Svalbard, and in the restaurant Dans le Noir? Once again, I found myself realizing that it made no difference if my eyes were open or closed. Naturally my eyelids closed: it was almost as if they recognized that they had no job to perform in that place, and could take time off for a while.

The period of floatation was introduced with some gentle music which faded after a brief time, leaving me with no sense of time or space. I felt enveloped, warm, cocooned. I drifted in and out of wakefulness, never fully sleeping but held for periods of time in that dreamlike state which precedes both deep sleep and a state of wakefulness—the state of the Theta brainwave, which is also frequently observed during times of meditation. At various points, I found myself thinking I was in bed, or floating in space, the effects of gravity having been apparently removed. I had read in the waiting room that as the stimulation of the senses is halted, there is a swift process of stress release, and I certainly emerged—even after one short session—feeling calmer and clearer-headed than I had done upon arrival. The effects are supposedly accumulative, however, and beyond being a mere marketing ploy, the anecdotal and scientific evidence does seem to point towards the increased benefits of regular floatation therapy, in which deep darkness is key.

Human responses to darkness vary, of course. For many, to enter the lightlessness of the floatation tank would be unthinkable, an utterly terrifying prospect. Ever since humankind discovered its capacity to inflict pain of the most ghastly kind upon its own race, the withdrawal of light has been used to inflict physical and psychological torment. The powerful and vivid hallucinations experienced by Sylvie Dymáková at Vila Mátma, as a direct result of her lack of optical stimulation, are commonly referred to as "prisoner's cinema", a term first used by those undergoing sensory deprivation as a form of torture. Yet there is something in the darkness which we miss at our peril. In our pursuit of and obsession with the light, are we in some sense disturbing the natural balance and rhythm of the universe, unsettling a God-given equilibrium which is reflected in the very nature of the world in which we live? Do our assumptions about the primacy of light over dark ignore some stark realities of life?

In the wider animal kingdom, darkness serves a fundamental purpose for many creatures: strange, twilight creatures with translucent skin, mole rats, and bats, none of which have need of light to see and navigate and sense. In fact, it is believed that around thirty per cent of species of vertebrates and sixty per cent of invertebrates are nocturnal.[72] At night time, underground, in the depths of the oceans, and in remote caves there is a whole plethora of life forms which need darkness in order to thrive. Although it is only in the last 300 years that artificial light has allowed human beings to enter into the night, animals have always done so. Many are specialized night-time dwellers, emerging at night in some parts of the world in order to avoid the intense heat of the day, adapted for the dark, predators with enhanced senses of touch and smell and hearing, for whom eyesight is of no importance. Creatures such as the three-toed sloth and the anteater rely on these senses both to avoid larger predators to whom they themselves would represent prey, but also to detect their own prey. Insect predators take advantage of the dark to catch other insects which stray and get caught in the threads of their larva. Owl monkeys in the Amazon rainforest leap assuredly through the trees as if it were broad daylight, aided by their large, glowing eyes which are fifty per cent bigger than those of other monkeys. Pink river dolphins use sound to navigate and hunt at night, their highly tuned sonar allowing them to be active in the total blackness of their environment. Unbelievably, many animals can live in the dark as easily as we live in the daylight, and whilst many are polyphasic, being active for periods during the day and the night, there are creatures which dwell entirely in the dark. In a cave in Venezuela, scientists and explorers have discovered creatures which are believed to have evolved in darkness over millions of years, never having been exposed to sunlight: swimming crickets with long antennae and sensitive pads for feeling their prey, enormous jaws, and spiny legs, all features which allow them to operate and function fully with no conception of light; a rare catfish with no skin pigment and eyes which seem to be disappearing because neither feature serves any function—the catfish navigates its way through the cave system using its enhanced whiskers, and its skin is covered in taste buds!

As far as the oceans are concerned, it has long been recognized that many forms of life thrive in their mysterious, murky depths, shunning light and hugging the ocean floor. A process called "vertical migration" describes the way in which various organisms—zooplankton, crustaceans, and fish—swim to the surface of the water during the darkness of night to feed. They then return to the bottom of the sea when the sun comes out. A recent research project undertaken in the Arctic[73] has revealed that the same thing happens during the Polar Night when it is dark all day and all night. These are truly dark-loving creatures, as even the tiniest amount of diffuse sunlight appearing in the middle of the day is enough to keep them near the bottom of the ocean until nightfall. Moonlight has also been observed to have a similar effect. The project has revealed that Arctic kelp can survive on just one week's sunlight. It stores the energy in this brief period in the summer but it actually grows during the darkest months of the year, when there is no light at all. Some forms of plankton algae, right at the bottom of the food chain, have even been shown not to need sunlight at all; they are able to create energy without the process of photosynthesis which most forms of the species normally need to survive. The Polar Night also harbours some bird life. It is commonly assumed that birds migrate away from the darkness of the winter months, and most do, but there are some which remain. The ptarmigan has long been known to remain in the darkness, but the marine life research project has revealed that it is not alone! Brunnich's guillemots and little auks have been spotted overwintering in the Arctic, seeking dark areas and avoiding places with light.

The recognition that such life forms exist challenges our way of thinking. Even within the human race there are, of course, vastly differing levels of visual perception—very few people have twenty-twenty vision. Some have lived in permanent darkness from birth, never having seen sunlight. Many more live with diminishing vision, having to get used to an increasingly darkening perspective. Those of us in that situation need some serious redefinition of the images we use; when darkness is normative, it cannot always be bad. And think, then, of the dense, lightless underground cradling the dormant seed back to life. Darkness may bring with it all sorts of associated practical difficulties, but who would dare to say it is not of the essence of life: necessary for life, not to be feared but to be respected, perhaps even longed for. We think that light is the source of life—yet it is in darkness that all living things have their naissance; in the womb, in the earth, in the sea, in the seed, in the tomb, the absence of light is necessary for life to take hold.

IV

In 2014, an exhibition of original masterpieces by Leonardo da Vinci was held at the ArtScience Museum in Singapore, the first time these works had been displayed in South-East Asia. The exhibition focused on the *Codex Atlanticus*, da Vinci's largest notebook. This would be the last time these pages would be displayed for a very long time. In an interview about the exhibition, its curator Honor Harger explained that the biggest enemy of such old drawings is light. After the three-month exhibition the works would need to rest in darkness for three years! Enter any gallery or historic property and you are likely to find low levels of lighting; sometimes you may even see a sign explaining that the lighting is kept at a particularly low level in that space in order to protect a specific artwork, exhibit, or item of soft or hard furnishing. Both artificial and natural light can cause breakdown and degradation of sensitive materials, although the high levels of ultraviolet radiation in natural sunlight make it the greater enemy. Watercolours and inks and all materials with a natural source are particularly susceptible, and works of art can crack and fade, sometimes to the point where the details and original colours are no longer visible as the dyes and pigments change and break down. Blinds and titanium films are used to cover windows to filter and reflect incoming sunlight, and artificial lighting levels are closely monitored. Conservation of historic works has become an exact science, with most modern galleries and exhibition houses devoting a significant budget to ensuring that the lit environment is appropriate for their works.

Yet it is not just works of art that are susceptible to light damage. Whilst light is, of course, vital for the overall health and fitness of humans—it is related to many aspects of our physiology, including the proper regulation of the body clock—various research studies have suggested that exposure to artificial light prior to sleep and during the night might be linked to depression, diabetes, obesity, and even breast cancer.[74] Depending upon the sleep patterns of any one individual, the fading of light is associated with an increase in the hormone melatonin, which anticipates the daily onset of darkness. It is not without good reason that it is known colloquially as "the darkness hormone"! Melatonin has the reputation of being something of a wonder hormone and any inhibition of its production, such as that caused by artificial light encroaching upon the normal circadian rhythm, can have a negative impact upon all those physiological and mental processes which its production regulates. One study reported that "exposure to electrical light between dusk and bedtime strongly suppresses melatonin levels, leading to an artificially shortened melatonin duration and disruption of the body's biological signal of night."[75]

It is the disruption of regular patterns of melatonin secretion that is also partially held responsible for the condition known as seasonal affective disorder (SAD). Many are familiar with SAD as a condition which affects some people during the dark and cold months of winter. The "winter blues" often begin with the onset of the autumn months, when the nights draw in and the weather—in some parts of the world—turns cold and damp. It is characterized by low levels of energy, a low mood, sometimes depression, extreme tiredness, and overeating. When spring appears on the horizon the mood lifts and a smile returns. It is only in the last thirty years that it has been acknowledged that SAD can also occur in the summer months. So-called "reverse SAD" impacts fewer than ten per cent of those affected by SAD but is nevertheless a recognized condition, returning at around the same time each year, again marked by increased anxiety and melancholy, although with some different symptoms from its winter counterpart as well—insomnia rather than oversleeping, weight loss rather than weight gain. It was a relief to me to know that I am not alone in dreading the onset of summer. I used to think it was just vanity, knowing I would never be "beach body ready", and I do not class myself as among the most chronically affected sufferers, but still I long for the winter and the excuse to hibernate that it affords. I retreat indoors in summer, or into whatever shade I can find, trying to avoid that sense of over exposure which it can be hard to avoid in the long hours of daylight. That I would choose to light a fire on a warm summer evening is perhaps less the result of an innate quirkiness attributed to me by my friends, than of a simple need to recreate the ambience of the colder winter months.

Just as the turning-on of a light at night can inhibit melatonin production and thus lead to depression, or potentially a whole manner of other conditions, so too the disruption of the body's natural light-dark rhythm through over- or under-exposure to sunlight at various times of the year appears to impact upon some people in an unambiguous way. We are back to balance. Not enough sunlight, too much sunlight, not enough darkness, or too little darkness, and the pineal gland which produces or ceases to produce melatonin in response to the external triggers of light and dark gets confused. Our physical and mental (and, I would argue, spiritual) well-being depends upon this balance.

Svalbard Journey
First Visit, 8 January 2013

I eat a meal with new friends at four o'clock in the afternoon. It's dark outside, of course; the restaurant is dimly lit, there are candles on the tables, and my instinct is to linger; this is a familiar scenario, one which goes with a slow pace and wine, well earned by eight or nine o'clock in the evening. Yet this is the middle of the day and it is a functional eating we share, drinking water and leaving as soon as we have taken food. No time even for coffee.

And then the opportunity to begin to talk to people about why I am here. There is no surprise, or bemusement, rather a gentle recognition and appreciation of my chosen theme, a consensus that

I had come to exactly the right place, and an eagerness to talk about the dark season.

9 January 2013

Of course life has to go on as usual. There are jobs to be done, children to be cared for, school to be attended, homes and relationships to be maintained, sleep to be had, and I wonder if—without the natural rhythm of the light and dark—there is a need to be more deliberate about these ordinary actions. I have just made a list of the things I plan to do tomorrow, and in what order and in which part of the day I will do them; this is more than simply an adjunct of my normal tendency towards OCD. It is a measure to prevent sliding into a continuous night-time and into that evening mentality of rest and recreation. It feels as if the dark season somehow forces a slowing down, a more leisurely approach. Although this may be as much, if not more, to do with the harsh weather conditions than it is to do with the restrictions of the darkness, it is clear that less activity is possible. I wonder how long—if ever—it takes to get used to the things which cannot be done. Does frustration persist or does it fade away as the darkness infiltrates the soul and becomes part of being? Perhaps the physiological impact of the lack of sunlight for such a long period is also a contributing factor, but there is definitely a feeling that energy is sapped at this time; not only is it necessary to move closer in to see the detail of the landscape, but people also move closer in to one another. I may be romanticizing but there feels to be an atmosphere of quiet conviviality. In conversation with a group of children in the church this evening I discovered that they were surprisingly enthusiastic about the dark season—most said they prefer the light time but a few said this is their favoured time of year. One girl said she likes playing outside in the dark best of all.

CHAPTER 6

The Creative Darkness

Light thinks it travels faster than anything but it is wrong. No matter how fast light travels, it finds the darkness has always got there first, and is waiting for it.

Terry Pratchett, from **Reaper Man**[76]

I

The account of the creation of the world with which the book of Genesis opens imagines the fundamental state of being as one of darkness. This cannot and should not pass us by! Before anything else, God dwelt in darkness (Genesis 1:1–2). Darkness, wind, and water were all that was—an ancient expression of Trinity perhaps; the fundamental elements from which all things were brought forth. In separating the light from the dark, "God saw that it was good." (Genesis 1:18). This earliest of accounts, drawn together as it is from strands of even more ancient myths and oral traditions, accepts the necessity of darkness as an equal partner with the light. There is no hint of the supremacy of one over the other; each has its own peculiar identity, the uniquely dark character of what was to become known as the night being protected by the creation of a "lesser" light to rule over it (Genesis 1:16). It is an account of the creation of a balanced universe, yet it is the darkness which is the mother of all, giving birth to the light, with God as the divine midwife. Jewish tradition to this day interprets the Torah as defining a day as beginning at sundown.

The acceptance of darkness as a divinely ordained state reappears later in the Old Testament through the voice of the prophet Amos, who announces, "For lo, the one who forms the mountains, creates the wind, reveals his thoughts to mortals, makes the morning darkness, and treads on the heights of the earth—the Lord, the God of hosts, is his name!" (Amos 4:13) and "The one who made the Pleiades and Orion, and turns deep darkness into the morning, and darkens the day into night . . . the Lord is his name!" (Amos 5:8). Psalm 104 offers a similar affirmation, verses 19–23 saying, "You have made the moon to mark the seasons; the sun knows its time for setting. You make darkness, and it is night, when all the animals of the forest come creeping out. The young lions roar for their prey, seeking their food from God. When the sun rises, they withdraw and lie down in their dens. People go out to their work and to their labour until the evening."

The narrative of a dramatic creation event happening *ex nihilo* (out of nothing) is common to a wide variety of cultures and religions (both monotheistic and polytheistic). In many of them this nothingness is explicitly described as a deep darkness, or night. As with the Genesis account, many of these myths describe a lone divine figure hitherto unseen and inactive, dwelling in the nothingness, who spontaneously and playfully speaks or sings a new world into being. One ancient account of creation, that of the Kiché people of what is present-day Guatemala, Honduras, and San Salvador, recorded in their annals the *Popul Vuh*, begins with the words, "Over a universe wrapped in the gloom of a dense and primeval night passed the god Hurakan, the mighty wind. He called out 'earth', and the solid land appeared."[77] Among the Native American Apache people, the story of creation sees four gods emerging from a primordial state of infinite darkness and void. As if from nowhere, so the story goes, a disc appears, upon which is seated Creator, the One Who Lives Above. As he gazes upon the darkness, light appears, then colour and clouds. Upon one such cloud sits Girl-Without-Parents and then, as Creator sings, so appear Sun-God and Small Boy, and so the rest of creation is gradually disclosed. There is then a great flood and the charging of responsibility for the creation to the Girl-Without-Parents. Eventually, Creator produces fire and, along with the other gods, disappears into the billowing wafts of smoke.

There are many other stories typical of this genre—I have chosen to offer just these two less well-known examples. However, their similarity to each other and to the first Genesis account suggests that the "creation from darkness by a divine being" motif strikes a cross-cultural chord, possibly tapping into a universal and innate sense of darkness as the source of all being. So powerful and alluring is the image that it has continued to be used into modernity. A contemporary allegory of creation, with which many readers will be familiar, is offered in *The Magician's Nephew* by C. S. Lewis (part of the *Chronicles of Narnia* series). When Diggory and his companions arrived in the place which was not yet Narnia, they encountered somewhere which was "uncommonly like Nothing. There were no stars. It was so dark that they couldn't see one another at all and it made no difference whether you kept your eyes shut or opened . . . The air was cold and dry and there was no wind."[78] Eventually, in the darkness, the lion Aslan sang the world into being.

Prevalent in folklore as a potent and creative force, darkness is the pure and sinless state from which beautiful and unanticipated things inevitably emerge. There is a sense of gestation, of the darkness welling up, holding onto its secrets until it can hold them no longer and they burst forth to form things new and complementary—light, life, and love. Counter-intuitively, and laying waste to the notion that darkness represents evil and light represents good, it is usually with the advent of light and form within these great myths that evil, ignorance, and selfishness also manifest themselves.

II

"Stars hide your fires, let not light see my black and deep desires." So reads the unattributed[79] quotation on a flyer I am handed somewhere along the River Thames one day in late summer. It is an advertisement for "Blackout: Step into the Darkness", a celebration of London's "dark river" being held as part of the annual Thames Festival. The flyer advertises a range of culinary and wine-tasting events, all with a dark or candlelit emphasis. From "starlit opera" and a "blindfolded banquet" through to "neon noir" and a "fire and flambé night". Something I have noticed in recent years—perhaps it is particularly an urban Western phenomenon but it is there nevertheless—is a trend towards cultural and community events in the dark. We are invited on postcards and posters for sale about town to "Seize the Night". In London it is possible to see Shakespeare by candlelight at the Globe Theatre. The Museum of London offers its visitors the opportunity to experience a "Night Owls Sleepover", spending the night in the museum in order to "hunt down history by torchlight". In Sydney, Australia, it is possible to listen to "Bach in the Dark", a concert of Bach's music played in the crypt of the city's oldest church. Charitable organizations now frequently hold "MoonWalks", a traditional sponsored walk but throughout the night rather than during the day. All manner of events are marketed with a dark or specifically night-time unique selling point. The treasures of darkness are being discovered, so it seems (or re-discovered!), as people are encouraged to free themselves from the distractions of light, to discover their inner creativity and passion, to see the world from a different point of view, and to connect more intimately, not only with the darkness itself but with their fellow revellers.

Once, when leading a retreat on the subject of darkness, I invited the participants to take a walk after dark. I asked them to pay attention to the darkness and to be aware of what emotions and feelings it evoked. The most powerful response came from a woman who described the walk as leaving her feeling "alive, layered, and calm". It is no wonder, then, that for centuries, darkness has been the muse of choice for creatives of all kinds as it sparks ideas, helps discover new things, and stills the heart. Painters, musicians, architects, poets, and actors have all been inspired by the darkness and within the darkness. Recognizing its inherent creativity, many have learned to manipulate it to create a whole variety of visual effects, successfully harnessing its power as a tool for generating texture, depth, and atmosphere in their work.

When I first saw the Northern Lights I was intrigued to notice that the shafts of light were not the penetrating shades of emerald that are usually portrayed in photographs. Rather, I observed them to be a paler grey—with a faint hint of green, yes, but nothing like I had seen on the cover of *National Geographic*! I was to learn that this is because the long exposure needed to take pictures of the aurora in the dark exaggerates the natural nocturnal colours. Even my own amateur attempts to capture the phenomenon on my mobile phone proved this. The colours in my photographs were entirely different—more vivid and intense than I had seen with my naked eye. The professional photographer Rut Blees Luxemburg specializes in photography after dark, believing that the nature of the images captured at this time offers a whole new perception of night. Rather than a time associated with fear, cold, danger, forbidden spaces, and threat, it becomes a time of seduction and life. The warmth of the colours created by the longer exposure times generates a whole new world which invites the observer to reconsider their often unfounded negative pre-conceptions of the night. Rut Blees Luxemburg's approach to photography has an esteemed forebear in Leonardo da Vinci who, long before the invention of the camera as we know it today,[80] also believed that the ideal time to create pictures was after the sun had gone down. At this time of day, he experienced a subtlety and delicacy of light which was most conducive for his work. His scientific mind understood that the reduced levels of natural light resulted in the dilation of his pupils. This, he recognized, opened up the possibility of seeing a much wider range of mid-tones in the palette.

There are other reasons why night-time is the right time for anyone engaged in creative activity. The sleepiness which comes naturally at eventide is believed to have a stifling impact upon cognitive function. As the capacity for critical analysis is impaired, so artistic tendencies are enabled to flourish and creative ideas allowed to come to the fore. In her book *It's Not Only Rock 'n' Roll: Iconic musicians reveal the source of their creativity*, Jenny Boyd writes about the way in which many of the musicians she interviewed found that they were at their most creative just prior to sleeping. She observes:

> For most people, near slumber is the time when the veil between
> the unconscious and the conscious mind is most transparent.
> With the body and rational mind at rest, the inner self is freed.[81]

So the romantic image of the tortured artist or writer working into the depth of night seeking inspiration possibly has some tangible physiological foundation after all! Practitioners of the Dark Retreat (see Chapter 5) have reported that as well as a general sense of physical and spiritual wellbeing, they have, after being immersed in total darkness for several days, entered into intense periods of creativity. Even people with no previously attested artistic abilities have written books, formed sculptures, and produced drawings whilst on the dark retreat, the imagination apparently freed as a result of the lack of optical stimulation. Whilst preparing this book I have, without doubt, written most easily and prolifically in Svalbard. As I write now, during this, my third visit, it is 2 p.m. I look outside the window next to my dimly lit writing desk and it is very dark. It may also be to do with the isolation and the quietness, but there is no question in my mind that the Polar Night frees up the creative waves in my brain and allows me to focus on my theme in a way that I have not experienced anywhere else.

Back home in London it is one hour earlier, and I am aware that my eighteen-year-old daughter may well not yet have risen to start her day. Anyone with a teenager living in their household may complain at the apparent lack of respect for conventional hours of rising and sleeping, but do not underestimate just what may be happening in terms of innovation and imagination! Teenagers love the night, but it may not just be an act of rebellion or the result of a newly discovered freedom. Scientifically speaking, the night-time is an inspirational time, the impairment of sleep liberating certain connections and ideas in the mind. So ventures into the early hours may be a necessary part of the personal and social development of the younger personality as it consolidates identity and self-awareness. At least, I will tell myself this next time Meg comes home at 5 a.m.!

Svalbard Journey
First Visit, 10 January 2013

Today, a conversation with some teenagers; with one or two exceptions they were clear about preferring the lighter time of year, but were also able to express a particular appreciation for this dark time—in particular its "cosiness" and associations with Christmas and New Year celebrations. There was indeed an acknowledgement that the body seems to slow down. For some this means that sleep comes more easily and readily, for others that sleep is hard to come by; either way the disturbance of slumber patterns can be accompanied by a sense of ongoing tiredness. This was not a signal for distress, however, rather simply a sign to take life at a more leisurely pace, to find recreation indoors rather than out, and to be less energetic than the lighter months allow for. There was no sense of this being a time of year which is dreaded or feared—when it is a part of life, the way of things, the way of nature, the dark, it seems, holds no fear.

III

I live in North London, but just occasionally I venture south of the river! This is not as easy as it sounds, and not just because of the traditional, if light-hearted, enmity between north and south Londoners. South London is commonly noted for its paucity of public transport. An exception to this, however—and a good reason for anyone to head across the Thames—is a London Underground station on the Jubilee Line. Designed by Sir Richard MacCormac and opened in 1999, Southwark tube station pays testament to the power of the deliberate use of light and shade in the design of the built environment. Deep underground, yet with the sky still visible from below, a forty-metre-long wall, comprising 496 triangular azure blue glass panels, is held in place by immense concrete supports. The glass panels reflect the natural underground darkness and the supports create dynamic shadows as the daylight streams in through the ceiling above. The shimmering blue tones and the contradiction of beautiful light in an underground cavern contribute to an overall effect which is one of theatre rather than transport hub, and of tranquillity rather than the chaos usually associated with a tube station. If you find yourself passing through between Stratford and Westminster, it's worth getting off at Southwark for a few minutes just to take in this architectural masterpiece.

Increasingly, it is being recognized that architecture has a lot to learn from visual art, especially when it comes to balancing light and shade, and making use of darkness as a starting point (or blank canvas) from which to make light appear. Just outside Osaka in Japan is Tadao Ando's Church of the Light. Built in 1989, the church is a simple, solid, minimalist concrete construction, the main feature of which is a giant cruciform window, its narrow arms and spine taking up the entire east wall. Throughout the morning, natural light pours into the naturally dark space, transforming it with light and shadow. Later in the day it is transformed again as the space reverts to a stark void. For the architect, these simultaneous distinctions—a designed duality—are key. Ando wants the observer to be brought to a greater awareness of the balance which is at the heart of all life.

There are, however, environmental as well as aesthetic reasons for rethinking the ways we design and light our buildings and urban environments. Looking at the earth from outer space at night, the outline and shape of the continents and the concentration of populations is clearly observable because of the proliferation of electric lighting. Yet we might ask why it is necessary for light to be so powerful that it can be seen from above the planet. It is, in effect, lighting up the sky—wasting light. With the advent and increased use of LED lighting it is possible to preserve darkness in a way that conventional lighting cannot, because it does not leak light—rather it focuses exactly where the illumination is needed. Urban populations have become very used to living with a high level of artificial light, yet it is possible to be gentler, to create environments that respect and appreciate darkness, and to contribute towards the overall health, well-being, and safety of the community.

In 2012, the famous London gathering point, Leicester Square, was given a total facelift. This included particular attention being given to the night-time appearance of the square and the ways in which lighting could be used to enhance the experience of visitors. This did not mean, however, that the lighting was designed to be as bright as possible. The designers responsible for the illumination project wrote, "In the past, the attitude of 'the more light the better' has led to a general abundance of light, especially in urban areas. We now know that it is crucial to rethink the value of darkness, to understand the different shades of night and to allow the night to have its own unique set of characters."[82]

It is widely accepted that places which are well lit are safer than unlit ones, but modern urban lighting designers are recognizing that this is only true to a certain extent, up to a certain level of illumination. Some experts have concluded that too much light at night reduces the capacity of the eyes to adapt to a darkened situation, making it harder for them to see potential dangers.[83] Too much lighting can, therefore, be a factor in reducing safety. On the other hand, lower, atmospheric lighting that plays with the darkness, enhancing it and making a feature of it, creating shadow and ambience, has the potential to attract more people which, in turn, contributes towards a safer environment. Managing to pay attention to both safety and aesthetics, the lighting design for Leicester Square at night has created a magical and popular setting, without simply re-creating the daylight. The night-time itself has become the canvas upon which a living, interactive, and contextual work of art has been created, and into which the observer is invited to enter, to embrace the different levels of darkness and the enchanting qualities of the time of day after dusk.

In 1933, the Japanese novelist Junichiro Tanizaki published his essay "In Praise of Shadows",[84] an exquisite meditation on Japanese aesthetics and architecture, and their deliberate use of shadow and darkness. Delightfully, his work contains an ode to dimly-lit Japanese monastic toilets as epitomizing this trend! He even goes as far as suggesting that the broody, shady atmosphere offered in these places of "spiritual repose"[85] has been the stimulus for many a haiku poet, and he laments the trend towards white porcelain fittings and shiny metal fixtures in modern domestic bathrooms. Lighting and roof design all play a critical part for Tanizaki in the establishing of a particular ambience which is conducive to a gentle daily living; he even writes about "the beauty of the alcove".[86] This description captures powerfully something of what I hope to convey in the Dark Creed (see Chapter 8) in appealing to the image of the shadow as a metaphor for the Holy Spirit. Tanizaki says:

> When we gaze into the darkness that gathers behind the crossbeam, around the flower vase, beneath the shelves, though we know perfectly well it is mere shadow, we are overcome with the feeling that in this small corner of the atmosphere there reigns complete and utter silence; that here in the darkness immutable tranquillity holds sway.[87]

Reading Tanizaki's essay has helped me to understand something about myself which has always troubled me (and one of my dearest friends, in particular). That is, why it is that I have an aversion to restaurants with crisply starched and pristine white table cloths and gleaming stainless steel or silver cutlery! I have always found such places, regardless of the quality of the food, to be soulless and devoid of atmosphere, generic, and lacking in imagination. It also helps me to rationalize my intense preference for pottery above glass, which is also a Japanese trait. He proposes that objects which have a translucent and cloudy surface, and which reveal a "sheen of antiquity"[88] or a "glow of grime"[89] resulting from years of touching and handling, bring to mind the past and carry within them the stories of those who have been part of creating their present appearance.

How real it is, this tendency to want to polish and sparkle, to wipe away, to see our own reflection in the crystal or metal, a tendency which demands that which is new and pure rather than that which is matured or blemished. Is it not the case that the sparkle of glass and the sheen of the metallic can appear tacky and intimidating with their apparent aspiration to perfection? Is it not also true that with a different eye and a different priority, things dull, with a shadowy, darkened, and imperfect surface, can be seen to encapsulate an intrinsic and earthly beauty rooted in life and reality rather than in what we imagine life *should* be like? I am reminded of a powerful song by the American singer-songwriter Danny Schmidt: "Stained Glass" tells the story of a small church whose prominent stained glass window of the crucifixion was shattered by the falling of an elm tree a month before Easter. The lyrics tell how the original artist is deceased but his father, by now an old man of ninety, agrees to do the restoration. Come Easter morning the window is unveiled, only to reveal a rough and grotesque reconfiguring of the original, described as "apocryphal and frail". As the light shines through the window the many imperfections in the glass and its new configuration are exposed, and the song concludes:

> God removed his veil to show the scars upon his face
> Some folks prayed in reverence and some folks prayed in fear
> As all the shades and chaos in the glass became a mirror[90]

Shade and light. Perfection and imperfection. These things cling together in a complex and shifting relationship, which relies upon their interplay to expose the full and true and perfect nature of God, which in turn reveals the full and true and perfect nature of humanity.

IV

Some of my favourite works of art are by the American artist Mark Rothko, whose large-scale paintings are characterized by immense, intense, and textured rectangular blocks of colour, often floating on a contrasting background. Many of them use bold, vivid colours but there is also a range of much darker paintings using a stark relief of grey and black. Rothko took his own life, and it would be very straightforward to conclude that these particular works reflect a bleak, depressive state. Of course, we can never know exactly what was in his mind as he created them, but the paintings do challenge the observer to consider the nature of darkness, in particular black, and its depths of shade.

In the 1960s, Rothko was commissioned by philanthropic art enthusiasts, Dominique and John de Menil, to create a series of paintings around which a new chapel would be designed and built. Eventually opened in 1967, the Rothko Chapel in Houston is an octagonal space displaying fourteen monumental works of art by the artist, each with a strikingly dark and sombre aspect. Yet they are not gloomy. The dim light of the chapel enhances and draws out the purple tones in the paintings, cleverly emphasizing the vision of the founder that the chapel should be a meeting point for art with the sacred, a place of meditation as well as a modern art gallery. Dominique de Menil said she saw it as "a gathering place of people who are not just going to debate and discuss theological problems, but who are going to meet because they want to find contact with other people. They are searching for this brotherhood of humanity."[91] Since its inception the Rothko Chapel has developed a reputation as a centre for the exploration of human and civil rights and interfaith dialogue, and the ambience generated by the Rothko canvases is key to this endeavour.

Suna Umari, a long-time servant of the chapel, says, "They're sort of a window to beyond . . . the bright colors sort of stop your vision at the canvas, where dark colors go beyond. And definitely you're looking at the beyond. You're looking at the infinite."[92]

There is a common piece of handed-down wisdom which says that on a hot, sunny day one should avoid wearing black because it absorbs the heat and light. To remain cool, so the insight goes, wear white. As a committed wearer of black, even in the height of summer, I have always sought to brush off this advice, telling myself I can remain cool, calm, and collected even in my traditional clerical shirt and cassock! However, there is a scientific basis for it which perhaps I should no longer ignore. Physics tells us that black is not actually a colour at all, rather it is what the eye sees when deprived of any visible light. Something appears black if it absorbs light, rather than reflecting it back so the eye can see. The more a substance absorbs light and the colour it contains, the blacker it appears. Hence the person wearing black in the sunshine becomes something of a heat magnet! Looking at it from a more artistic perspective, black can be created by merging the three primary colours, which themselves combine in varying degrees to form every other shade the eye can see. Whichever way you look at it—black as the absorber of all colour, or black as the combination of all colour—black takes on a richness and depth which belies its immediate, austere appearance. So it is possible to see within the dark paintings of Rothko not a harsh and uninviting gloominess, but rather work which incorporates and holds everything that ever was, and ever will be. In this way they become images of hope and possibility. Rothko's exploration and treatment of dark colours offers a delightful opportunity to consider their nature, to look below the surface, and release ourselves from the shackles of preconception.

Other artists have concentrated on work which explicitly contrasts darkness with light. In the art world, the Italian term *chiaroscuro* (literally "light-dark") is used to define the technique which balances light and shade in order deliberately to create an impression of three-dimensional volume within a two-dimensional space. Chiaroscuro—which uses bold and strong contrasts and emphasizes tone and brightness rather than colour—has resulted in some of the most magnificent, emotionally evocative, dramatic, and visually appealing paintings ever produced.

The master of the technique is generally regarded as Rembrandt, who has been nicknamed "the master of light and shadow", although the technique first became recognized when it was used by Leonardo da Vinci. Caravaggio is another artist renowned for his skilful deployment of the technique. Chiaroscuro works by illuminating a central point within the painting—a figure or object—at the same time as obscuring the surrounding background. By darkening the canvas, a single shaft of light or a single spot can be brought into dramatic focus, drawing the eye of the viewer and creating an enhanced atmosphere. Actions take on a greater intensity and figures appear stronger, more passionate, and mysterious. Faces, such as Rembrandt's own, depicted in "Self-Portrait as the Apostle Paul" painted in 1661, are richly ingrained with shadow, focused around the eyes, cheeks, and mouth, creating a sense of introspection; the viewer cannot help but wonder what the subject of the painting is thinking! One of Rembrandt's best-known paintings, and a superlative example of the method of chiaroscuro, is his "Adoration of the Shepherds", painted in 1646 (though possibly by one of his pupils). The painting depicts a traditional manger scene, with the Holy Family surrounded by shepherds and other figures held mainly in shadow. One of them holds a lantern, yet the main light source in the painting is the Christ child himself. In this powerful work, the light emanating from the baby in the foreground represents not only a profound artistic gesture, but offers a point of theology from the painter: here is the one who is to be the light of the world.

It is important to recognize, however, that the technique of chiaroscuro demands an analysis which goes beyond the assumption that the light is purely and simply there to draw the attention of the viewer away from the darkness. It might be tempting from a theological point of view to define chiaroscuro in this way—that its purpose is to allow light to shine over and against darkness, dispelling it, and standing as a metaphor for goodness amidst a bad darkness. However, this is a technique of balance which demands that the viewer explore the darkness and shadow as much as the light, for they are, in their complementarity, responsible for the beauty of the work. Rembrandt's painting of the nativity captures the nature of chiaroscuro most poignantly. Yes, we can only see the true glory of the child when the light is lowest, but the almost total blackout of the background scene takes us into the reality of this new-born's existence; he is not the light fighting against the darkness, he is the one who balances all things, who holds both light and dark, exuding light and dwelling within darkness at the same time. For the chiaroscuro artist, darkness is a positive force on the canvas, used to enhance meaning and emotion. The darkness of the painting demands that we look at *it* too, to see it as the foundation of the mystery and life of the painting, in which things are not only unseen, but are also seen differently, through a different lens.

In the Baroque era, in which Caravaggio and Rembrandt were painting, the world of theatre also began to discover the powerful impact of darkness and shadow, just as public street lighting was becoming more commonplace. Many of the special effects which remain central to French and English theatre and Italian opera emerged in this period, based on the new-found possibility of completely darkening the environment and then manipulating the darkness with focused lighting to create visual effects.

Also around this time, in the state of Kerala in southern India, a new art form was developing. Kathakali (literally meaning "dance-drama") is a rich, passionate, and colourful form of theatre, usually performed within the temple compound as an act of worship, telling tales of gods, spirits, and demons. Its roots go back to even earlier traditions of folk ritual, dance, and hand-to-hand combat. Fundamental to a Kathakali performance is the fact that it starts after sunset, with the audience called gradually into the theatre by the playing of traditional drums. As night falls, so the play begins as the actors enter the performance space. The Kathakali stage is a simple, bare platform with none of the peripheral infrastructure common in Western theatres—wings, backstage, scenery, curtains. Just a simple stool suffices as the only prop, used by the central actor for whatever purpose suits the occasion, along with a moveable screen which is used to introduce new players onto the stage. In the very front of the podium stands a large lamp with a thick wick, the Kali-vilakku, or "dance-lamp". This lamp, which emanates a natural yellow light, is topped up with coconut oil as and when necessary, and its primitive and simple nature means that the light it sheds creates a focal glow. In other words, the luminosity is focused in one small area of the stage. Although the beam moves according to the wind in a natural rhythm, it attracts and focuses the audience's attention within this concentrated circle of light, even as the drama unfolds. In a living, moving show of chiaroscuro (although it would not be called that!), actors use the lamp as a tool to emphasize changes in emotion and mood. By sitting directly beneath the lamp, fine movements in the face are simultaneously highlighted and shadowed by the movement of the flickering flame, which would traditionally have been the only source of light. The performance of Kathakali at night is significant in that it symbolizes the rich world of magic and fantasy which the art form embraces. The combined twilight and sleepiness allow the viewer to enter more readily into that world, the aura of which is only broken with the coming of the dawn, when the performance conventionally ends. In recent years, Kathakali has mainly been performed for the tourists and travellers who flock to the lush south-west Indian state. Whilst the essential elements remain, including the use of the lamp and an insistence upon no fixed or static lighting at all, the resolve of the spectators does not usually stretch to an all-night performance! The few remaining authorities and authentic practitioners lament the loss of this essential, aesthetic dimension of the art form, seeing the heart of Kathakali as beating most strongly in the middle of the night.

An even older form of theatre, with its origins in the fourteenth century, Japanese Noh drama also places great emphasis upon darkness and shadow. In a similar vein to Kathakali, Noh relies upon a dark atmosphere and candlelit stage in order to convey an other-worldly setting. In its own portrayal of creation mythology, Noh theatre is characterized by stories of gods or ghosts often emerging from a womb-like darkness. Actors wear masks which, although fixed in appearance and apparently lacking in any obvious expression, can be manipulated to convey a wide range—it is said an infinite range—of facial expression. The subtle changes in emotion which can be portrayed are dependent upon the breathing patterns and the angle of the head and body of the actor, background music, and scene context, and most importantly here, the use of shadow. A simple lift or bow of the head subtly shifts the shadow and changes the countenance, influencing the way in which the observer understands and recognizes the expression. Here, strangely, we come full circle to Leonardo da Vinci. Anyone fortunate enough to see his masterpiece, the "Mona Lisa", cannot help but be mystified by the way in which her facial expression changes depending on the angle from which the portrait is viewed. From a peripheral angle she appears to be grinning. When viewed from head-on she seems more serious, scornful even. Perhaps even more than the question of who the woman in the painting actually is, this is the conundrum which has challenged art experts and tourists alike.

However, a study into the way that shadows alter the facial expressions of Noh masks[93] has offered an interesting explanation. The study concludes that the manipulation of shadows on Noh masks can significantly alter the way in which emotions are recognized. This, the researchers suggest, also offers an explanation for the elusive qualities of the Mona Lisa's smile. Their hypothesis is backed up by more recent research from Sheffield Hallam University,[94] which has concluded that a painting technique known as "sfumato" is responsible for the strange effect in Da Vinci's most famous work. *Sfumato* means "soft" or "smoky", and the artist uses a method of blending delicate colours and shades—in the case of the Mona Lisa, around her mouth—in order to create a discreet yet noticeable optical illusion. Leonardo is well known for his use of this technique, once writing that light and shade should blend "without lines or borders in the manner of smoke".[95] His commitment to creating gentle, gradual shifts between light and dark means that it is impossible in much of his work to determine where shadow ends and object begins, and in this way the smile of his most famous subject appears to shift in a mysterious and illusory way.

V

The people of Longyearbyen in Svalbard celebrate the ending of the Polar Night with a Sun Festival. As the sun first peeks its way back over the horizon in March, a whole variety of events—both secular and sacred—take place over the course of a week to welcome its return. Such is the sense of delight that you could be forgiven for thinking that the ending of the period of Midnight Sun would be greeted with dismay, fear, or sadness. Far from it. The people of Longyearbyen also celebrate the impending Polar Night, only this time they celebrate with a music festival: in particular, a blues festival, "The Dark Season Blues". Returning to Svalbard for a third time at the start of November, when the darkness is almost completely formed, apart from a few remnants of twilight in the middle of the day, I am captivated by the talk of the impending season. There is a genuine sense of anticipation as the people look forward to the months ahead and to the slower pace and quieter, more subdued life they bring. Blues music seems to capture well not only the mood of the season but also its colours. As the light gradually disappears day by day, the blueness of the environment becomes exaggerated. With great subtlety, it moves through a whole palette of shades ranging from a dusky, almost royal-hued blue when the sky is clear and the light just still visible, through the grey-blue shades of the atmosphere when it is heavy with ice-rain or snow, to the deep navy blue of the clear dark sky. Artists from all over the world come to take part, helping the local community to make the transition from bold, bright, active, and lively, to calm, shaded, relaxed, and still. The emotional rawness of blues music, encompassing as it does a wide variety of emotions, makes it a natural herald of the dark time of the year.

So it is not just the visual arts which find inspiration in darkness and night-time. I am reminded, as I contemplate the connection between blues music and darkness, of the move made by one of my favourite singers, John Grant, who relocated to Iceland because he found the dark months to be particularly creative and inspiring for him as a songwriter. Although the title of his album *Pale Green Ghosts* actually refers to the olive trees which grow near his family home, I find it hard not to believe that somewhere in his memory and imagination there is an image of the Aurora Borealis, so visible in Iceland and so perfectly described in that one expression. In 2014, the BBC was moved to make a documentary with Grant, called "Songs from a Dark Place". The programme explored music from Iceland and celebrated the way in which "a land deprived of sunlight for so much of the year has become the focus for a melting pot of musical creativity."[96]

Songwriters and musicians of all genres have been moved to create powerful and positive lyrics reflecting the sensual, intimate, and mysterious qualities of the dark, lauding it as a time and place for finding stillness, for dreaming dreams, and for making love. From the powerful blues of Ray Charles declaring that "The Night Time is the Right Time" to Louis Armstrong's classic jazz ballad "What a Wonderful World", and Billie Holiday's "Romance in the Dark", songs the world over have been written in praise of the darkness and the night. Even as you, the reader, are digesting these words it is not unlikely that you will have found a particular song coming into your mind, so numerous and well known are the examples!

Christian hymnody, however, is somewhat less sympathetic to darkness as it falls back, time and time again, upon the prevailing imagery. Hymn books are packed with poetry extolling the virtuous light and its power to overcome or banish darkness. So universal and persistent is the imagery that we take it for granted, the paucity of positive dark-related images going unnoticed. Here are a couple of examples which appear in many commonly used hymnals:

> God, whose almighty word
> chaos and darkness heard,
> and took their flight,
> hear us, we humbly pray,
> and where the gospel day
> sheds not its glorious ray,
> let there be light!

> Spirit of truth and love,
> life-giving, holy Dove,
> speed forth your flight;
> move on the water's face,
> bearing the lamp of grace,
> and in earth's darkest place
> let there be light![97]

It pains me to admit it as a good Methodist, but even Charles Wesley is guilty of the unholy equation in this well-loved hymn:

> Christ, whose glory fills the skies,
> Christ, the true, the only Light,
> Sun of Righteousness, arise,
> triumph o'er the shades of night.[98]

As I write, the season of Advent is upon us and I am struggling to find hymns suitable for this period of the liturgical calendar which do not force me to compromise the heart of what I am trying to convey in my script. So entrenched, in hymns old and new, is the imagery of Christ, the light, coming into the dark world, that it is, I would venture to say, an addiction. This modern Advent Candle-lighting hymn by John Bell—beautiful as it is—is typical of the genre:

> The first is for God's promise
> to put the wrong things right,
> and bring to earth's darkness
> the hope of love and light.[99]

As is this by Graham Kendrick:

> Darkness like a shroud covers the earth.
> Evil like a cloud covers the people.
> But the Lord will rise upon you
> and his glory will appear on you,
> nations will come to your light.[100]

It is not that there is anything wrong *per se* with these hymns. In fact, many hold within them a deep poignancy and poetry. As I have said, it is not my aim to dismiss the image of Christ as light. I mention them simply to draw attention to the fact that there are very few hymns which offer a counter-balance. One which does is the hymn by Laura Story and Jesse Reeves describing an amazing God which asks the question:

> Who imagined the sun and gives source to its light
> yet conceals it to bring us the coolness of night?[101]

Margaret Rizza comes close to the theology espoused in this book as she writes:

> In the darkness of the still night,
> in the dawning of the daylight,
> In the mystery of creation,
> Creator God, you are there.[102]

As does John Glynn:

> I watch the sunset fading away,
> lighting the clouds with sleep.
> And as the evening closes its eyes
> I feel your presence near me.
>
> I watch the moonlight guarding the night,
> waiting till morning comes.
> The air is silent, earth is at rest –
> only your peace is near me.[103]

Thankfully, Charles Wesley redeems himself and offers balance with his image of God's presence residing in shadow and cloud in one of the greatest hymns of all:

> Captain of Israel's host, and Guide
> of all who seek the land above,
> beneath your shadow we abide,
> the cloud of your protecting love.[104]

I am thankful for all those hymns which attend to the beauty and blessing of night and the God-given qualities of darkness. I have mentioned some of them here, if only to encourage the reader to seek them out, to search for others, and to be consciously aware of the overwhelming and influential narrative offered by most of the hymn collections available today.

Moving into yet another musical genre, the foremost classical work which offers a positive outlook on darkness is Karol Szymanowski's Symphony No. 3, Op. 27, *The Song of the Night*. In a dramatic and sensual setting of the poem of the same name by the thirteenth-century Persian Sufi poet Jalal al-Din Rumi, Szymanowski offers a work which challenges preconceptions about the night-time as a place of fear and dread. In three movements, the composer conjures up the atmosphere of Rumi's middle-eastern night: warm, exotic, and fragrant, with dark skies illuminated by a myriad of stars. This is a night of chosen wakefulness, a night to be aware of being in the presence of the Divine, although the language, as with much of Rumi's poetry, takes on the characteristics of a lover speaking to the beloved. A solo tenor takes on the voice of Rumi's poem, singing in deep and reverent praise of the night, but also standing in awe of it, in profound silence. The singer is accompanied by an ethereal choral refrain which sustains the sense of mystery and profundity of the piece, representing perhaps the paradox of the poet, struggling to remain awake yet, at the same time, experiencing the deep joy and sense of elation which comes with a tangible sense of God's presence. Andrew Huth, in his programme notes for a performance of the symphony by the BBC National Chorus of Wales and the BBC Symphony Chorus, part of the BBC Proms Series in 2014, described the work as like "drowning in music . . . one of the most intoxicatingly sensual scores ever composed."[105]

The Song of the Night

O, do not sleep, beloved, through this night!
You, soul of my desire, I thirst for you.

Bid sleep begone this night!
And let the great mystery be revealed.
You are Jove,
roaming the starry sky this night.
Soar like the eagle!
Set free your soul in the firmament!

How still it is! All asleep . . .
and I alone with God!
What ecstasy! God is awake,
and I with Him this night!

If my eyes should blink before the dawn,
then shame on them, to lose a moment of this night!
Behold the starry thoroughfares,
when those on earth are silent! Our night is their glittering day!
Leo and Orion,
Andromeda and Mercury gleam blood-red this night.

Baleful Saturn glowers
and Venus floats in golden veil!
Tongue-tied in the silence,
I need no words to sing this night!

Jalal al-Din Rumi[106]

It is the very nature of darkness to create. It cannot stop itself. Darkness has an artistic soul and a divine heart which sings and writes and paints and builds and dances beauty into being. This is the meaning of co-creation; the hand of God shaping and forming things from a void, using, in the creative process, the lives of those who have their own origins in darkness, which is every one of us.

Svalbard Journey
First Visit, 10 January 2013

After church this morning I was taken by the hand by one of the congregation and pulled outside, suddenly and urgently, where a strong strand of light was visible beyond the mountains. The sun was not yet above the horizon—and would not be for many, many days—but still its power to illuminate could not be held at bay. "Look," I was told with not some small degree of vigour, "the light is always stronger than darkness." After the day's events I reflect somewhat differently. Not that the light is stronger than the darkness, but rather, that light needs darkness to live—we cannot see light for what it is without the dark. Yet darkness can live alone, without light, as the fundamental state of things from which creation sprang.

CHAPTER 7

The Political Darkness

Dost thou also take a pleasure in us, dark night? What holdest
thou under thy mantle, that with hidden power affects my soul?

Novalis[107]

I

In 1664, the British captured a commercial fortification on the southern
coast of what is now Ghana (then called Gold Coast). The fort was
renamed Cape Coast Castle, and for over 200 years it was the primary
seat of the British administration in that region. But the "castle" also
served a far more sinister purpose. Gold Coast had become a centre of
the global slave trade. Captured inland, local men and women became
the most valuable commodity as they were taken to the coast to be traded
for weapons, cloth, sugar, and spices. Prior to their exportation to the
Caribbean and the Americas on board slave ships, the prisoners were
held for up to three months in the castle. Dungeons were constructed
especially for the purpose, holding up to 1,500 people at any one time.
The separate male and female dungeons were kept constantly in the dark,
only the narrowest shaft of light permeating the underground caverns
during daylight hours. There were no toilet facilities to speak of, and so
faeces, urine, and menstrual blood covered the floors upon which the
slaves sat or lay, crammed in, as though their captors gave them no more
care than battery chickens.

Like the concentration camps at Auschwitz and Dachau, Cape Coast
Castle serves as a permanent reminder and symbol of humanity's capacity

for inhumanity. That such places should become "tourist attractions" is a striking anomaly, yet there can be no doubt of their power to strengthen moral resolve for such acts of horror never to be repeated. I was prepared for my visit. I was prepared to be shocked. I was prepared to weep. What I was not prepared for was the impact which the darkness in the Cape Castle dungeons would have on me. It was a caustic, dense, threatening darkness through which the smells of the past seeped into the back of my throat and the pit of my stomach; smells of gut-wrenching toxicity which represented the utter dehumanization of such enforced humiliation. It was a darkness which continued to hold the sounds of incarcerated and shackled bodies, catching me off guard 300 years later and making me want to place my hands over my ears as well as my nose. The capacity of darkness to enhance the senses is just as real in a place of squalor as it is in a place of beauty.

There can be no doubt that darkness was a primary weapon in the arsenal of degradation, leaving the slaves disorientated and confused, rendering them passive and lethargic. The small shaft of light would have been a cruel and tantalizing reminder of the life and relationships from which they had been permanently severed. Then, having spent up to three months in near-total darkness, the humiliated and tortured souls were eventually led through the "Door of No Return". Hurtled suddenly from their sensually deprived incarceration into the strong African sunlight, they were temporarily blinded, their eyes having become accustomed to the constancy of the darkness. Following in their footsteps, albeit with a tour guide and low artificial illumination, it was a light which, even with modern sunglasses, still burnt into my eyes after just a few minutes in the dungeon. Any captives who chose to put up a fight were thrown into a separate cell—above ground but with no natural light whatsoever. This cell for "recalcitrant" or stubborn slaves was essentially a tomb in which they were left to die in pitch darkness, the scratched grooves on the floor bearing testimony to the desperate and cruel nature of the death. Our guide pointed out the incongruity of the luxury accommodation on the floors above in the Governor's quarters—sixteen windows for one person, with awesome views of staggering natural beauty; views out to sea across a route to captivity and death.

I could not write this book without acknowledging that darkness—for all its delights—takes on a very different identity when used as a weapon. The transatlantic slave trade may seem to be located deep in the past, but its repercussions are still tangible in the modern world, and for many people, darkness—in different ways—is still used to threaten, to instil fear, and to dominate. It has the capacity to marginalize and oppress. Conversely, light is associated with power and privilege. At the start of the industrial age, the choice to lie in bed late into the morning was the preserve only of those who could continue their daily activities later in the evening by costly artificial light. And still, in the modern world, heat and light are political; like water, none should be without them, yet many still are. It is an imbalance of power made starkly visible from the air once it is dark. Fly over parts of the developing world at night and witness first-hand the discrepancy between densely populated and permanently lit urban conurbations and dark, barely lit rural areas in which people live, but without connection to a grid or the means to run a generator. Around one fifth of the world's population are believed to be without access to electric light. According to the then UN Secretary General Ban Ki-Moon, "widespread energy poverty still condemns billions to darkness, ill-health and missed opportunities for education and prosperity."[108] Even in many cities across the world, electricity is unstable and artificial light consequently unreliable. Governments are unable or unwilling to do what is necessary to ensure the provision of regular and dependable power, and such administrative apathy and state neglect inhibits the development and educational advancement of some of the world's poorest communities. Especially for women, electricity (and, in particular, electrical lighting) equates to empowerment.

"I cannot help but wonder how many medical catastrophes have occurred in public hospitals because of 'no light,'" writes the Nigerian novelist Chimamanda Ngozi Adichie, reflecting in *The New York Times* on the problems created by the unstable electricity supply in her native country. She continues, "how much agricultural produce has gone to waste, how many students forced to study in stuffy, hot air have failed exams, how many small businesses have foundered? What greatness have we lost, what brilliance stillborn? I wonder, too, how differently our national character might have been shaped, had we been a nation with children who took light for granted, instead of a nation whose toddlers learn to squeal with pleasure at the infrequent lighting of a bulb."[109]

Even in London where electricity is reliable, it is not uncommon for someone to come into church asking for money to "top up" their electricity card. For those on lower incomes, the traditional pay-as-you-go meter has been replaced by a top-up card; but like a meter, once it runs out of money, the power is cut.

In any community, loss of electric light can equate with increased danger. At the start of 2015, the Office of the United Nations High Commissioner for Refugees began a campaign (in partnership with the Swedish home furnishing chain IKEA) to raise funds to purchase LED light bulbs to improve living conditions in its refugee camps. Giant banners on display in IKEA stores proclaimed, "Refugee communities deserve to socialise after dark" and "Refugee families deserve to feel safe after dark". The IKEA Foundation donated one euro for every LED light bulb or lamp sold in stores or online, each euro being the cost of one LED light bulb for the camps. Refugee camps are often complex, chaotic places and after sundown many basic actions such as walking around, collecting water or food, and going to the toilet become more problematic and less safe (more so for women and girls). If the camps cannot be lit artificially then opportunities for refugees to retain some semblance of normality and dignity through working, reading, learning, socializing, and moving around the camp freely are severely compromised. Refugee camps harbour certain dangers when night falls.

Seemingly a world away, the streets of London are also home to many refugees, who face a very different kind of night-time trial. In the winter months they join the numbers of men and women for whom the night, in spite of its artificial light, represents a time of risk and vulnerability. It is not uncommon for those who are forced, for one reason or another, to inhabit the night to be the subject of physical violence or verbal abuse. These are folk already weakened by homelessness, poverty, poor mental or physical health; people living in an unfamiliar context and not speaking the local language; sex workers, those down on their luck. It is not uncommon for any of these individuals to find themselves the victims of random attack. Ironically the same people, not appearing to have any purpose for their after-dark excursions, can themselves be prone to being stopped by police as potential villains, especially if they are running, begging, or simply look a certain way.

From the late thirteenth century in urban England, it was illegal to be out on the streets once the daily curfew had been announced by the ringing of church bells. The purpose of the curfew was primarily two-fold. Firstly, it offered a framework within which civilized society could function, respecting the natural biological rhythms dictated by daylight and night-dark. Secondly, it was a matter of social order and class: the curfew presented a legitimate opportunity to apprehend and rid the streets of all those who were considered (justifiably or not) to be a threat to polite and respectable living. By definition, this meant that it was legislation which gave validity to sexist and racist ideologies (many of those considered a threat and removed from the streets after dark were sex workers or Jews) as well as being adversely inclined towards those ostracized from the mainstream by disability. People of the distinguished classes, even if their motives for being out at night were less than wholesome, tended to be immune from detention, whilst those of the lower classes were assumed to be up to no good, regardless of their intentions—the men assumed to be drinkers or thieves, the women prostitutes.

Whilst in the West the curfew has not been normative since the advent of street lighting, legislation against walking the streets at night remained on the statute books in the UK until the 1960s. Although the law had not been enforced for many years prior to that, the world of "post-circadian capitalism"[110] continues to this day, albeit unconsciously, to classify, label and distinguish between those who use the night legitimately and those for whom it is a place of misadventure, a place of illicit activity, or a place to hide. In the early hours of a weekend morning, the vibrant East London neighbourhoods of Shoreditch and Dalston are teeming with people enjoying the bars, restaurants, and clubs for which the area has become renowned. Mostly the crowds are good-natured and high-spirited, but there is also an element of anti-social behaviour, anything from urinating or vomiting in public spaces to physical and verbal aggression. Street Pastors and Community Police Officers patrol these and other similar areas, offering support to those who, usually as a result of excessive alcohol consumption, are not quite in control of their behaviour and bodily functions. Yet these are mainly young professional adults who, come Monday morning, will report to work or turn up at university, their banter and behaviour justified as youthful high jinks, and tolerated as the unavoidable downside of the economic benefits which their presence brings to the area. Cheek by jowl in the same streets, mingling yet rarely mixing, are those who are disenfranchised by the night-time economy, hoping to benefit from it by receiving the metaphorical (or possibly literal) scraps from beneath the table. These are the ones who are looked upon with disdain and sometimes fear, passed by, insulted, ignored, prone to being arrested or "moved on". In his book *Nightwalking: A Nocturnal History of London*[111] Matthew Beaumont helpfully distinguishes between two terms used in the Middle Ages, "noctivagation" and "noctambulation". Unsurprisingly, noctivagation has the same Latin root as the word vagrant (*vagare*, meaning to wander) and refers to the activity of those who are forced to use the night as a place to seek refuge. On the other hand, noctambulation refers to the activity of walking at night with purpose and reason, deemed to be the domain of the respected and advantaged. Whilst these are terms which have long since vanished from common use in the English language, the division to which they draw attention remains a reality. The street at night continues to be a difficult place to be if you are without money, a place to stay, or anyone who cares.

Ride the night buses across the city and you will find it is possible to meet people from all over the world, who for one reason or another are seeking sanctuary from a night-time without shelter or support. As Bryan Palmer has said, "The night has always been the time for daylight's dispossessed—the deviant, the dissident, the different."[112]

Many years ago Abdul came to the UK seeking asylum, fleeing communal violence in Gujarat, India. His asylum claim was refused, meaning that he had no recourse to public funds. He stayed with friends for a while but was unable to do this indefinitely. With no alternative support network, he became homeless and destitute. Abdul volunteered in the kitchen of a charity which gave him some food and travel expenses. He used the money to buy a London Travelcard so that he could spend the nights riding the extensive network of twenty-four-hour buses which cross the city. This is his account of the experience of night-time bus riding:

Every night I used to go on a different bus. Nighttime I started about eleven o'clock. Bus number 25 Oxford Circus to Ilford, it is one and a half hours. In this one and a half hours I was just sitting on the chair napping. This is the longest ride. At the last stop if I didn't wake up they were saying, "This is the last stop, get down." If I didn't get down maybe they call sometimes the police. Sometimes if the driver is nice maybe they let you in. Otherwise I stop at the last stop and waited for another bus. I get the bus and go on another route. Sometimes I'd go to West Croydon, sometimes I'd go to Heathrow, sometimes I'd go to Golders Green. So all the different parts of London in the nighttime I was taking a bus. If I take four journeys then my night is finished.

Sometime nighttime is difficult and dangerous because they try to rob you. Once they took my Travelcard and my £20. It was very difficult, I had to walk from Ilford back to Oxford Circus during the nighttime. All the time I changed bus routes. Upstairs I used to sleep at the last seat when it was not busy. Lots of people sleep like that in the bus. Particularly the weekend was very difficult for me because on Friday and Saturday all people finish at one o'clock or two o'clock and I couldn't sleep. During the winter, it was very difficult, in the cold. I passed a whole winter, over five months, like that in the bus.[113]

After one year sleeping on buses Abdul gained access to a hostel and he continues to volunteer with different organizations supporting other refugees and migrants. His experience, however, highlights the stark contrast that exists in the depth of night between those who are forced into it without means or purpose, and those for whom it represents a well-resourced lifestyle choice, a time and space of leisure in which life and friendship can flourish.

Whether resulting from a lack of artificial light or a lack of choice, prolonged enforced darkness can in no way be a source of delight or joy. At its worst it can be terrifying, debasing, and death-inducing. Only if a person's basic needs are met can it be possible to find the greater sensual riches of life. Only then can darkness be that place of healing and regeneration in which life is nurtured and love is made.

II

Across the world in recent times, women's organizations have sought to reclaim the night as a positive space. Gathering and protesting after dark, often holding lighted candles, the "Take Back the Night" or "Reclaim the Night" movement is seeking to redefine the night as a safe space, especially for women. After dark has always been a time of fear for women, a time associated with violence, in particular sexual violence. The movement demands changes in attitude, behaviour, and law so that women can move freely in their communities without fear of attack, being able to use the night to their advantage, for their own ends, and for life-giving and life-saving purposes, rather than being subject to life-denying activity.

As I write, a terrifying situation is unfolding as hundreds of thousands of refugees are making their way from war-torn Syria, trying to reach safety in Europe. A devastating civil war has led many citizens to flee in fear, taking their lives and those of their families in their hands as they seek, by whatever means they can, to migrate to a better life. Many have drowned at the hands of unscrupulous people-smugglers, trying to cross the Mediterranean in boats which sink because they are not fit for purpose or have been overcrowded. Others, realizing the inherent dangers in the sea crossing have attempted to travel by land, crossing through Turkey with the aim of eventually reaching Germany, Sweden, the United Kingdom, or other places of perceived safety. Some countries have closed their borders, feeling unable to cope with the vast migration, leaving swathes of people stranded—old and young, able-bodied and disabled—unable to return home or move forward. A few compassionate border guards, however—recognizing the potential for death on a massive scale—have tried to find ways of helping people across. In a move reminiscent of the Underground Railroad movement of nineteenth-century America, or those two nights in which the Danes helped nearly all their Jewish population to escape to Sweden as the Nazis arrived, under the cover of night people have been smuggled across the border on their way to freedom.

The Underground Railroad was the name given to a complex but well-organized system of secret passages, safe houses, routes, and meeting points used by thousands of slaves to escape from bondage in the South to the free states of the North and Canada. Places that were willing to shelter runaway slaves were "stations" or "depots". Those who organized the shelter were called "stationmasters" and those who assisted the movement of people from one place to the next were the "conductors". But in spite of this infrastructure, for many of those trying to escape it was not necessarily straightforward to know where to go. There were no road signs helpfully proclaiming the way to "The North"! One of the main strategies—having made the initial escape from their owners, usually under the cover of night—was to locate and follow the constant North Star. "Keep your eye on the North Star" was the advice because by keeping that star in sight, up ahead, the runaway slaves could be sure that they were heading in the right direction. Of course, this meant always moving at night. But how to be sure they had located the correct star? I was always taught to identify it by looking for the saucepan with a bent handle—an easier description to understand than the formal Latin name of the group of stars, Ursa Major (Big Bear). The runaway slaves were taught to look for the constellation that looked like a drinking gourd—it was common at the time to use a hollowed-out gourd to drink water, and these were supposed to look like long-handled cups. Those planning escape were told, "Two stars on the cup's edge always point to the North Star." There is even a traditional song, "Follow the Drinking Gourd", which describes this and other signs used by people escaping to the North:

> The riverbank makes a very good road
> the dead trees show you the way
> left foot, peg foot, traveling on
> follow the drinking gourd
>
> When the sun comes back and the first quail calls
> follow the drinking gourd
> for the old man is waiting to carry you to freedom
> if you follow the drinking gourd

The allegory of the Exodus of the Hebrew people from Egypt at night was always held at the heart of the Underground Railroad movement. Harriet Tubman was known as the "Moses" of her day. Acting as a conductor on the railroad, she guided hundreds of slaves to safety over a period of about ten years. Araminta Ross (she only later changed her first name to Harriet) was born into slavery. From her early childhood she worked as a servant in the house of her masters, and later on in their fields. She eventually married a free black named John Tubman and took his last name. In 1849 she learned that many of the slaves on the plantation where she worked were to be sold and she took the decision to run away. Helped by a local sympathizer, she set out under the cover of the night, following the North Star, and eventually made her way to Philadelphia. There she was able to find work and save some money, at which point she made the brave decision to return to the place of her enslavement to rescue some of her family. This she did successfully, and she returned again and again to the South to rescue many more people. The night was always a valuable companion to Harriet Tubman and to many other escaping slaves, offering a blanket of cover and a star to guide. Although written in the later era of the struggle for civil rights in the US, Paul McCartney's song "Blackbird", and its image of a blackbird with broken wings singing in the night as it learns to fly, offers a powerful metaphor, borrowed from the literal night-time flights to freedom of the Southern slaves decades earlier.

As dangerous and threatening as it can be, darkness holds within it a great capacity for subversive activity. During the Vietnam War the Viet Cong lived in vast complexes of underground tunnels, which were carefully and deliberately crafted and used in order to defy the military might of the US. From within this subterranean darkness, victory was achieved. I am also reminded of the miners who were at the forefront of the Labour movement in 1970s Britain. Can their prominence in the struggles for workers' rights that characterized and dominated the politics of that era be at least partially explained by the solidarity and camaraderie which inevitably developed among groups of men toiling away deep below the surface, locked into close relationships in claustrophobic coal seams?

Darkness has a political heart, beating in time with those who are willing to put their lives at risk to change the world. God has entrusted darkness into human hands, but many times we have let God down. We have betrayed God and we have betrayed the darkness itself, turning it from the friend it seeks to be into a death-inducing enemy, allowing it to be imprisoned by the forces of evil and used against God's ultimate purposes of justice and freedom. Yet even in the midst of war and degradation, darkness reaches out to offer whatever helping hand it can, calling us to trust it and to follow, saying, "Sometimes only the darkness will do." We owe it to darkness to reach out and grab that hand. To respect what it has to offer. To join it to the hand of the light, that united in a common yearning for a new politics and a new integrity we can explore and utilize the richness of the resources they both have to offer.

Svalbard Journey
First Visit, 8 January 2013

Mining is the basis upon which the community of Longyearbyen was founded, and the evidence and detritus are visible all around. Vast, creaking icons of a bygone age are scattered across the landscape like giants frozen in time. How beautiful they are in their industrial and utilitarian style. I am reminded that darkness is the stuff of life for miners, shaping an existence almost impossible to understand for those of us who live our lives above ground: a community of enforced intimacy, fostered within the cocoon of the earth; a shared toil from which emerges the deep bonds of brotherhood. Yet mining in this place takes on a different dimension. Perhaps during the time of the Midnight Sun there is relief to be found in retreating beneath the rock face to labour, but during the Polar Night I wonder what it must be like to work underground all day in darkness—endeavouring, slogging, uniting, to the point of exhaustion—and then to emerge, into darkness still, but a different darkness. Are miners better prepared to cope with the constant dark, more attuned and prepared for the season, more able to slow down and to see things clearly, or do their bodies develop an instinctive association, Pavlovian style, between labour, sweat, and darkness, which makes the time of the Polar Night a difficult one to navigate?

CHAPTER 8

The Dark Creed

So fear not, my friend.
The darkness is gentler than you think.

Ben Okri[114]

I

I believe in God,
the creator of darkness,
who conceived of its potential,
and allows it to live.

I believe in Jesus Christ,
the prince of darkness,
who raises a canopy of grace
to shade the startled ones.

I believe in the Holy Spirit,
the inner shadow,
who clings to our soul
and distorts the shape of our sorrow.

The story of the Dark Creed begins in 1985, when my eyes were opened, my heart "was strangely warmed"[115] and a proverbial penny dropped. I left university in June of that year, and thanks to a well-connected chaplain, within a matter of days I had begun working in the magnificent County

Hall on London's South Bank as a Grants Officer with the Ethnic Minorities Unit of the Greater London Council (GLC). Ken Livingstone was the head of the council at that time and Paul Boateng (now the Rt Hon. the Lord Boateng) was the Chair of the Ethnic Minorities Committee, under whose auspices I was working. My role was to assess and monitor grant applications from community organizations and to write reports for the committee, recommending—or otherwise—the award of a grant. These were the last months of the GLC, condemned as it had been by Margaret Thatcher, who found herself threatened and undermined at every turn by a radically left-wing council in the capital city, the very existence of which mitigated against her conviction that there was no such thing as society. In order to process the outstanding grant applications and to ensure that there was as little money as possible left in the pot when the axe finally fell, a number of casual staff, myself included, were taken on to complement the existing staff. It meant that we had a flexible and generous brief, and in a little over one year I was inducted into a world of diversity and culture that astounded even a reasonably streetwise girl from East London like me. This was the pinnacle of the era of what was (misleadingly) being called "political correctness". In actual fact, it was a time when the subtly insidious and potentially dangerous impact that language can have began to be seriously (and rightly) acknowledged.

Like darkness and light, language can affect how we feel about things. It has the capacity to inspire or to undermine. It can delight or it can anger. It can offer affirmation or it can utterly destroy our sense of self. When a whole section of British society was self-identifying as "black", it became problematic and offensive to use the word as a negative metaphor. The colour black had a strong and long-standing symbolic association with death and mourning, and all things bad or morose (the wearing of black clothes at a funeral or the hoisting of a black flag at an execution, for example). Conversely, the colour white carried with it associations of purity, peace, and love. Specific metaphors which were commonplace in the English language served to underline or emphasize the evil of black: black magic, black moods, blackmail, blacklisting, the black book; even the word blaggard—meaning a rogue or a villain—is a colloquial spelling of "blackguard". A certain use of language became identified as one of the mainstays of a racist society, and conscious efforts were made over a period of many years, with only limited success, to retrain people into a different manner of expression. Some missed the point of the exercise entirely and, unable to distinguish between metaphor and description, believed that it was no longer possible to talk about black coffee or a blackboard! Others ridiculed the sociological shift and adopted the term "political correctness" as a way of diminishing the significance of the challenge, claiming a superficial purpose for the exercise rather than a deeper underlying one related to respect and identity. Indeed, although much did change, a stubborn refusal to accept that the use of particular metaphors could be connected to racist ideology and discriminatory behaviour was characteristic of this period. In his book *What Language Shall I Borrow?* the hymn writer and theologian Brian Wren says:

> Language, like tobacco, is habit forming. Some patterns of writing and speaking are addictive and may damage both the user and others who breathe the same linguistic atmosphere. If we see the damage being done and decide to kick the habit, we may get withdrawal symptoms and hostility or derision from other smokers. But in the end, we shall enjoy breathing fresh air.[116]

It took me a while to realize how I had been suffocating, but I did eventually breathe the fresh air, although my conscientization was formed the hard way. In one of the first reports I presented to the Ethnic Minorities Committee, proposing a grant to a group supporting the Grenadian community in London, I made reference to the US "intervention" in Grenada in 1983. Little did I know the storm I was unleashing, and in the use of that one simple word "intervention" I was torn to shreds. It was, I was told in no uncertain terms, not an "intervention", but an "invasion". I know that now. I understand the distinction now. But at the time, to appear to be in any way supportive of the Reagan administration's actions in relation to the small Caribbean island, to suggest in any way that the actions had somehow been invited, was sacrilege. I left the council chamber in shame, fighting back the tears, and suffered an agonizing elevator ride with the unforgiving gaze of the head of the Ethnic Minorities Unit and the chair of the committee bearing down upon me. In my harsh dressing-down, in my humiliation, I began to understand something of what this whole issue of language meant to people and why it was so important. I understood for the first time the nonsense of the old adage, "Sticks and stones may break my bones but words can never hurt me." In what I had written I had caused genuine hurt, and I needed to understand why that was.

Being surrounded by, and introduced to, so many people who were confronted on a daily basis by racist attitudes and prejudice allowed me to absorb the importance of the discussion, and in spite of my naïve mistake, perhaps even because of it, the use of inclusive language became a priority in my own self-development. So when, seven years later, I began training for the ordained ministry and was introduced to the framework of feminist and liberation theology, I was a sponge ready to lap up the ideas of scholars and activists such as Elisabeth Schüssler Fiorenza and Dorothee Soelle. I read books such as *In Memory of Her*[117] and *The Strength of the Weak: Toward a Christian Feminist Identity*,[118] and I began to understand something of how traditional Western theology and doctrine had been nurtured in the cradle of patriarchy. Their work encouraged me to think more broadly and to be able to recognize and challenge some of the hegemonic systems which had shaped the development of doctrine, the interpretation of Scripture, and the structure and practice of the Church. I instinctively identified with their critiques of the systems of power which had been in play over centuries in the Western Church. I felt empowered by the permission their academic credentials offered to a humble student such as myself to begin to reinterpret and redefine everything about the tradition of which I was so integrally a part. In particular, I was fascinated by their concern for a more inclusive approach to the language of metaphor that is used in an attempt to describe God. I had never recognized a problem with the idea of God as a Father. But then again, my own experience of being fathered was entirely positive. I would never want to lose that image. But what about God as mother, God as lover? Yet another world was opened up to me, and the writing of Brian Wren on this subject remains formative to this day. In the book referred to above, Wren explores the language that is used in talking about God. He uses the acronym KINGAFAP (the King-God Almighty-Father-Protector) to define the images which are normatively used to describe God. He explores the role of metaphor in theology and the importance of finding alternative metaphors in order that the whole of human experience might be reflected in our hymnody, liturgy, preaching, conversation and "God-talk". And it is in the pursuit of this objective, in pursuit of a "theology of balance", that I came to write the Dark Creed.

II

"I find people confusing." So says Christopher, the teenage boy living with Asperger's Syndrome, who is the central character in Mark Haddon's novel *The Curious Incident of the Dog in the Night-Time*. He continues:

> This is for two main reasons. The first main reason is that people do a lot of talking without using any words . . . The second main reason is that people often talk using metaphors. These are examples of metaphors
>
> I laughed my socks off.
> He was the apple of her eye.
> They had a skeleton in the cupboard.
> We had a real pig of a day.
> The dog was stone dead.
>
> The word metaphor means carrying something from one place to another . . . and it is when you describe something by using a word for something that isn't. This means that the word metaphor is a metaphor. I think it should be called a lie because a pig is not like a day and people do not have skeletons in their cupboards.[119]

Christopher has hit on something here! Whilst I would not want to go as far as he does in pronouncing metaphors lies, yet neither do they reflect concrete truths. That is not their purpose. Metaphors are mini-stories, brief images intended to convey an idea, an emotion, an aspiration, or a belief; they are not descriptions of fact. They are largely subjective descriptions which will work for some and not for others. Yet within the Christian tradition there are certain metaphors which have become virtually incontestable. The traditional Creeds of the Church—in particular the Nicene Creed and the Apostles' Creed—contain within them symbols and metaphors which have for centuries been repeated and imbibed up to the point where they have become absolute statements. As with Christopher, there is a tendency to believe that they reflect a literal and supposedly factual sequence of events, and to acknowledge that they do no such thing is perhaps the skeleton in the Christian cupboard! The Nicene Creed—constructed in the fourth century CE and perhaps considered to be the foundational statement of belief for the majority of mainstream Christianity—has become for some Christians what Luke Timothy Johnson in his book *The Creed: What Christians Believe and Why It Matters* describes as "an instrument of coercion rather than a glad expression of faith, a monument to the church's power rather than a movement of the Holy Spirit."[120] Although Johnson argues for a wider and more integral use of the Creed, he does not believe that it needs to compromise free-thinking and imagination, and over the years many writers have sought to offer alternative, contemporary creedal statements and affirmations of faith, attempting to encapsulate metaphorically and literally particular elements of Christian belief, whilst remaining within the broad traditional framework.[121]

The *Shorter Oxford English Dictionary* defines a metaphor as "a figure of speech in which a name or descriptive word or phrase is transferred to an object or action different from, but analogous to, that to which it is literally applicable."[122] Sometimes a metaphor is searched for. In other words, we think about the characteristics of the person or object we want to describe, and we look for a suitable image to describe them. Sometimes it is the nature of a metaphor itself which suggests or reveals characteristics of an object which had not previously been considered. I think it was the latter of these which led to the emergence of the Dark Creed in my mind. As I began to acknowledge some of the physical and emotional reactions which darkness stirred within me, I was reminded of God and of God's activity in my own life. As I began in later life to reach longingly for the shade rather than the sunlight, for night rather than day, for winter rather than summer, I found myself questioning the deeply ingrained Christian metaphors, and needing to express them in a way which could give expression to my relationship with God, the One who had created me, the One whose very humanity offers me a path in life, and the One whose energy bubbles within me and connects all things. Brian Wren says that "the best God-metaphors are those that move us deeply and enable us to encounter or be encountered by the dynamic dance of incandescent love that Christian experience names Trinity."[123]

If I understand what he is saying here, it is simply that if we are to capture the details, the nuances and the complexities of diverse humanity's pondering on the nature of the Divine, then a whole range of metaphors will be necessary. If a metaphor has the capacity to move us and to connect with our experiences in such a way that the nature of God is revealed more fully and profoundly, then it is a successful metaphor. The relationship between culture and experience and metaphor is what determines whether or not any particular metaphor "works" in any particular context. Many metaphors will be only partially successful, holding and describing some characteristics of the thing they are being used to define; they may also hold other, perhaps stronger, characteristics which are in tension with the object of the metaphor.

Such, for me, was the case with the metaphor of light in a Christian context. There is much to commend it, much to commend the description of Jesus as light. Think for a minute about all the things which light does and all the different sorts of light which exist; ordinary everyday lighting helps us to see what we are doing; street lights guide us and help us not to get lost; flashing lights offer a warning and tell us to be careful; the soft glow of candlelight offers us comfort and reassurance; Christmas tree lights, sparklers, and birthday cake candles are a sign of celebration. The message of Jesus Christ can offer all these things to those who embrace it. Yet bright lights can prevent us seeing, and even the dimmest of lights can inhibit rest. It is not for me a universally successful metaphor.

On the other hand, I also found myself questioning the insistent association of darkness with those negative elements of life which must be overcome and destroyed. Yes, darkness is fearful, it can prevent us from finding our way, sinister things happen at night. Yet darkness also comforts, and is conducive to rest; it challenges us to find alternative ways of doing things, it is associated with love-making and the growth of a seed. In the case of the Dark Creed, it is my intention to reflect something of my experience of the intimate nature of God, from within a traditional Trinitarian structure, but in a way that draws focus away from the metaphor of light and introduces the complementary metaphor of darkness. In doing so it is my hope, taking serious account of George Orwell's argument that "uncritical acceptance of existing phrases can shape thinking and hinder new thought,"[124] that I can draw attention to some imagined characteristics of the divine nature which have hitherto been obscured.

I have shown the Dark Creed to many people and most, in all honesty, have struggled with it, so universal is the metaphorical equation of light with good and dark with evil. Yet I offer it still, as a genuine attempt to open up a new way of perceiving an aspect of God's nature that works well for me. I still like and use the metaphor of light, but it has shortcomings and we limit God if we limit the metaphors we use to describe God, especially if we limit them to those which make us feel comfortable. Again, Brian Wren:

> Images of God in language must not become idols. However hallowed by tradition, however enriching and suggestive, however profoundly they move us, our metaphors and names for God are not themselves God. We should no more bow down and worship mental and linguistic images of God than the graven images forbidden in the Bible, or the idols of money and success.[125]

So having revealed some influences and described my own personal journey in getting to this place, I need now to attempt to unpack some of the metaphors I have used within the Dark Creed, which to many may seem strange.

III

I believe in God,
the creator of darkness,
who conceived of its potential
and allows it to live.

Earlier chapters have explored much of what lies behind this first stanza of my Dark Creed. Chapters 2 and 6 make reference to God as the creator of darkness; or at least, as the one who chose to retain darkness after drawing the light from it. God saw that darkness could serve a purpose in the ongoing story of humankind. The creation myths were generated from among peoples who understood the value of darkness, its necessity, and its possibilities. In their telling of the story of humankind and its relationship with the Divine, they placed the story of the creation of darkness into God's hands. The choice in the Dark Creed to emphasize the creation of darkness rather than of light is an attempt to respect those early storytellers, who could have placed the creation of darkness into the hands of a sinister force but instead chose to make it of God's doing. They chose to make it sacred. In the modern world, as in the distant past, the search for that which is sacred is the search to uncover the presence of God's nature in things, and in order to do that we need to be constantly rethinking and asking questions. Not everything is sacred—war and racism, for example, do not reflect the nature of God—but still God works within these things. There has been a tendency to assign darkness to the list of those things within which God works but which is not "of God". It is at the heart of the purpose of this Creed—indeed of this book—to challenge that assumption.

Svalbard Journey

First Visit, 22 January 2013

The shades of darkness seem almost infinite. From deepest black to a whiteness which in spite of its tone retains the character of the night. The palette shifts imperceptibly as the seconds and minutes pass by. Only over the course of hours can the transitions be noted, and over the course of a week there is a certain period of noontime light during which the duskier shades fade away day by day as the return of the sun draws closer. Tomorrow I shall awake in the morning light of London. The idea carries both a melancholy air and a sense of mystery. I have almost forgotten what the sunlight is. For sixteen days I have basked in the continuous sundown of the Polar Night, awoken to darkness, passed my days in darkness, and slept through darkness. The rhythm of life has been dictated by routine and relationship rather than any dark/light association. I find myself fearing the inevitable pace and exposure which light-time insists upon, yet I also want to see the details and the faces again. And in the end I want balance: the balance which I suppose was in the imagination of God when God drew forth the light from the dark. We can only know the beauty or the terror of a thing when we know its obverse. The light shines in the darkness, and the lightness does not overcome it.

IV

I believe in Jesus Christ,
the prince of darkness,
who raises a canopy of grace
to shade the startled ones.

There is something playful here, something deliberately mischievous about taking a tried and tested metaphor for the Devil and realigning it with the second person of the Holy Trinity! Shock tactics perhaps, and certainly some who have been confronted with this new association have been shaken by it. The phrase *princeps tenebrarum*—leader/ruler/prince of darkness—is believed to have appeared for the first time in a little known fourth-century text, *Acta Pilati* ("The Acts of Pilate", also known as the Gospel of Nicodemus), in which it is used to refer to Satan as Jesus descends into hell to liberate those held there. It is next known to occur in a hymn, *Rhythmus de Die Mortis* ("Rhythm of the day of death"), written in the eleventh century by the Benedictine monk Pietro Damiani (later St Peter Damian). In the words "*Cadat princeps tenebrarum, cedat pars Tartarea*" he offers a description of the Prince of Darkness as the yield of Tartarus. Tartarus was part of the Greek underworld, a realm of torment and punishment.

In the twelfth century, Bernard of Clairvaux uses the expression in his *Sermones in Cantica Canticorum* ("Sermons on the Song of Songs") and then in the seventeenth century, in English, the phrase re-emerges in Shakespeare's *King Lear* (Act III, Scene IV, line 140) and John Milton's epic poem *Paradise Lost* (Book X, line 383), in this segment:

> Whom thus the Prince of Darkness answered glad:
> "Fair daughter, and thou, son and grandchild both,
> high proof ye now have given to be the race
> of Satan (for I glory in the name,
> Antagonist of Heaven's Almighty King),
> amply have merited of me, of all
> the Infernal Empire, that so near Heaven's door
> triumphal with triumphal act have met,
> mine with this glorious work, and made one realm
> Hell and this World—one realm, one continent
> of easy thoroughfare. Therefore, while I
> descend through Darkness, on your road with ease,
> to my associate Powers, them to acquaint
> with these successes, and with them rejoice,
> you two this way, among these numerous orbs
> all yours, right down to Paradise descend;
> there dwell and reign in bliss; thence on the Earth

> dominion exercise and in the air,
> chiefly on Man, sole lord of all declared;
> him first make sure your thrall, and lastly kill.
> My substitutes I send ye, and create
> plenipotent on Earth, of matchless might
> issuing from me: on your joint vigour now
> my hold of this new kingdom all depends,
> through Sin to Death exposed by my exploit.
> If your joint power prevail, the affairs of Hell
> no detriment need fear; go, and be strong."[126]

Thus the "Prince of Darkness" gradually made its way into the popular imagination of the English language. One of many interchangeable names (the Devil/Lucifer/Beelzebub/etc.), it is most frequently used to refer to an archetypal malevolent figure who rules over Hell and has the capacity to influence human behaviour and society to move in the direction of evil. In popular Western culture it is also used more playfully as a tongue-in-cheek nickname for certain public figures who are perceived to have something of the "demonic" about them. The idiosyncratic rock musicians Ozzy Osbourne and Marilyn Manson, and the politician Peter Mandelson (with reference to his involvement in the Blair government's support for an invasion of Iraq in 2003) have all at various times been assigned this title. It is perhaps not quite so easy to understand its assignation to the inspirational jazz trumpeter Miles Davis, but that may just reflect my own penchant for his exquisite music; he did record a track of that name and he was renowned for his moody nature and unwillingness to be seen smiling.

In arguing for a more fluid and subjective approach to the use of metaphor, it is also interesting to note that the name Lucifer is more closely related to light than it is to dark! The name—which is Latin in origin—can be translated as "bearer of light", "day star", or "morning star", and the key to its ending up as a pseudonym for the Devil lies in ancient Babylonian mythology and the Old Testament book of the prophet Isaiah. The context is the exile of the Israelites to Babylon, and the belief of the Babylonians that the parents of their king were the gods Bel and Ishtar, who were closely associated with the planet Venus. The proximity of Venus to the sun means that it appears in the sky just before sunrise, and since ancient times it has often been ascribed the name "Morning Star". So the King of Babylon, believed to be a divine descendant of Venus, was himself called the Morning Star. In Isaiah 14, the prophet describes how God will restore the people of Israel to their own land, and how at that time they will taunt the King of Babylon and celebrate his fall from power and grace. When being translated into Latin, the title of the Babylonian king appeared as "Lucifer" and, in time, the sarcastic tone of the writer was lost; verse 12 was believed to refer not to the fall of an earthly king from a metaphorical heaven into a metaphorical pit, but rather to the fall of Satan from Heaven. Hence the name Lucifer came to be widely ascribed to Satan. More modern translations into English use the original sense of Lucifer; the NRSV, in particular, conveys the intended sarcasm well:

> How you are fallen from heaven, O Day Star, son of Dawn! How you are cut down to the ground, you who laid the nations low! You said in your heart, "I will ascend to heaven . . ." But you are brought down to Sheol, to the depths of the Pit. Those who see you will stare at you, and ponder over you: "Is this the man who made the earth tremble . . . ?"
>
> *Isaiah 14:12, 13a, 15–16*

In drawing attention to Lucifer's strange origins, I am merely making the point that metaphors can often carry hidden and unexpected truths. If Lucifer, the Prince of Darkness, is actually the bearer of light, the bright Day Star, then why can't Jesus, the Light of the World, be the Prince of Darkness?! By associating the term "Prince of Darkness" with the second person of the Trinity, I am appealing to those characteristics of darkness which offer respite and renewal. If we can associate darkness only with evil, fear, and death then it makes no sense to claim Christ as its Lord. If, however, we can associate darkness with creation, new life, and nurture, then it takes on a new potency as a metaphor for the One who can lead us to the resurrection moment of hope.

The canopy of grace is the knowledge of God's constancy being raised over us, allowing us to find calm and quiet and rest in the face of a glaring hopelessness. It is the relentless unconditional love of God which offers shelter and shade in the face of those things which startle or shock us, or leave us feeling—to use another powerful image—like a rabbit in the headlights! It is the love which comes most often through the touch of another human being, through the Christ-like activity which mirrors Christ's own self-giving love. It is the love made known in everything which affirms the presence of the Kingdom of God in the here and now. It is the love which takes seriously the discipleship imperative to pursue forgiveness, reconciliation, and peace. It is the love which takes our lack of direction, our human capacity for self-deprecation, and our tendency to panic in the face of the unexpected, and leads us to seek within ourselves and in one another opportunities for repentance and change.

V

I believe in the Holy Spirit,
the inner shadow,
who clings to our soul
and distorts the shape of our sorrow.

As this book has taken shape over several years, I have used for my note-taking a "Book of Shadows" in which to record my thoughts, ideas, and incessant musings. In the charming Cornish coastal village of Boscastle, home to the fascinating and only slightly kitsch Museum of Witchcraft, there are several of what I affectionately call "witch shops". It was in one such shop that I bought my *Book of Shadows*: a hard-backed notebook with blank pages crying out to be filled, with a black cover, plain except for a silver pentangle. Inside the notebook, a slip of paper informed me that "This *Book of Shadows* is a magical journal, or diary. A book in which to record your own magical path, in your own hand. Your journey is your own, this book is but a tool to help you along that path. By sunlight, by moonlight. Blessed be." The symbolism of the pentangle is similarly innocent. A five-pointed star representing the four elements and the four directions with a fifth point, the one pointing directly upwards, representing the sanctity of the spirit. All five points are bound with a circle representing the harmonious association between them all. The *Book of Shadows*, as well as the shop from which it was purchased, might at first glance, to the casual and unimaginative observer, be written off as a bit "New Agey". I am, at best, tolerated by my family when browsing the shelves of crystals, candles, angels, and all manner of paraphernalia which crosses well over the fine line between spirituality and fantasy. Much of what is on offer, though, does in fact provide a glimpse into a bygone era when the quest for divine knowledge, the sanctity of the earth, and the belief in the connectedness of all things defined the spiritual life of the people. Female "healers" wrote in their *Books of Shadows*—so called not because they were filled with sorcery and evil curses, as might be supposed, but rather because these personal journals, bursting as they were with rituals, spells, recipes, and other magical information, placed these women (who were essentially the homeopaths, therapists, and counsellors of their day) at great risk. If their writings were found they would face death, hence they had to be secreted in the shadows in order to avoid discovery. Hidden away, the depth of wisdom, intuition, spiritual understanding, and experience contained within them was protected for the present and future generations: a subversive and strangely liberating act, which stood in defiance of a misogynistic and patriarchal society that sought to contain wisdom and power within the hands of a few.

Shadows are surely capricious things! They have the capacity to transform and to defy as well as to soften, refine, and define, and to add nuance to the most ordinary scene or object. Shadows have the capacity to reveal the nature of the very thing they obscure. It has been said that the only interesting photograph is the one with lots of shadows. Cast upon the landscape, the shadows of clouds create patterns and shapes which alter the picture entirely, creating colours and movement and offering a window into the artistic imagination. Depending on the time of day and the angle of the sun, the human shadow can make us seem fat or thin, tall or short, elegant or deformed. There is even a tradition in ancient Sanskrit which teaches that it is possible to tell a person's destiny from the length of their shadow! Before noon we chase our shadows which go before us, after noon we are stalked relentlessly, our mysterious companion refusing to fade from sight until the sun finally bows down. In his poem "A Lecture upon the Shadow", John Donne uses the changing shape and

position of the human shadow as the sun moves in the sky to reflect upon
the shifting pattern of romantic love:

> Stand still, and I will read to thee
> a lecture, love, in love's philosophy.
> These three houres that we have spent,
> walking here, two shadowes went
> along with us, which we ourselves produc'd.
> But, now the Sunne is just above our head,
> we doe those shadowes tread;
> and to brave clearnesse all things are reduc'd.
> So whilst our infant loves did grow,
> disguises did, and shadowes, flow
> from us, and our cares; but now 'tis not so.
>
> That love has not attain'd the high'st degree,
> which is still diligent lest others see.
>
> Except our loves at this noone stay,
> we shall new shadowes make the other way.
> As the first were made to blinde
> others, these which come behinde
> will work upon ourselves, and blind our eyes.
> If our loves faint, and westwardly decline,
> to me thou, falsely, thine,
> and I to thee mine actions shall disguise.
> The morning shadowes weare away,
> But these grow longer all the day;
> but oh, love's day is short, if love decay.
>
> Love is a growing, or full constant light,
> and his first minute, after noone, is night.[127]

It is the shadow which perhaps best encapsulates the mutual dependence
of light and dark, sitting as it does in the cusp between the two. A little over
a year after originally visiting Svalbard, I retraced my steps to participate

in the church's special liturgy in celebration of the return of the sun. By the beginning of March the visible daylight lengthens by forty minutes in each twenty-four-hour cycle, hurtling at an alarming pace, and shifting the Arctic world, in a matter of weeks, from the total darkness of the Polar Night to the perpetual light of the Midnight Sun. It was good to be in Longyearbyen at a time of crossover, when there was both a dark night and a light day, and to have the opportunity to observe some dramatic patterns of playful light above and between the mountains. As I watched a shifting shard of late-afternoon light sink gradually down over Hjortfjell, where we had earlier celebrated the Eucharist as the sun appeared in the east, I realized that the beauty of the moment was neither in the light, nor in the shadow, but in the interplay between the two. Like the *Yin* and *Yang* which can only exist in their counter-play, it is a meaningless enterprise to try and discern if it is the shade which allows us to see the light or the light which helps us to see the shadow. We are spellbound more readily by the light, drawn under its hypnotic spell more readily, as it flutters its radiant eyelashes and beseeches us to "Look, look, look at me and see how brightly I shine!" Yet like the wind beneath the proverbial wings, the shadow drifts along, humble, yet full of self-confidence, secure in the knowledge that the light would be nothing without it. The shadow is, of course, already used widely as a tried and tested metaphor for a place of quiet and hidden support. Any individual who might be considered to be "in the limelight" usually has a team of people "in the shadows"; people who support actively but namelessly and upon whom the more prominent person relies utterly. Sometimes the person in the shadows is, themselves, waiting to burst forth, waiting for the opportunity to fulfil their potential. So, in its inherent beauty and encompassing of balance, and in its offer of sanctuary, sustenance, and possibility, I hope it is clear why the shadow is for me a viable and evocative metaphor for the Holy Spirit.

I am, however, conscious that some readers will be steeped in the Jungian notion of the human "shadow side", those undesirable and negative aspects of our unconscious which remain deeply buried. The image of the "inner shadow" will also, I know, for some people evoke the idea of a cancer. I have already made the point that few metaphors, if any, are universally satisfactory and all I can offer is the thought that, even as we skirt around the edges of our mortality and wholeness, we can hold fast to the belief that God is with us—a different kind of shadow. Our infirmities and ailments are not created by or caused by an interventionist God who rains down affliction as punishment for sin; such explicit nonsense has no place in the Christian gospel which speaks unequivocally of a God of love and redemption. Yet the possibility of God being—somehow—in the centre of that which strikes at our safety, welfare, and happiness, gently accompanying us, and moving with us on the often tortuous path towards and beyond death is one which speaks to the experience of many and the hopes of most. Faith does not remove our sorrow, but it can heal our soul. Holding and sensing an awareness of God's spirit—however we define that—is not a panacea for those things which cause deep misery and pain and distance us from the source of our wellbeing. However, it can, over time, "distort the shape" of heartache. Think of what a human shadow does! Its distortion of our body shape is often comical—it exaggerates our bad features or sometimes flatters us. Sometimes it creates grotesque shapes which mean we don't recognize ourselves. But underneath it all we know that we are the same person. Intense grief and a sense of loss never vanish, neither should they, yet it is possible to find a way of living with them. Sometimes at the height of grief we lose ourselves in raucous laughter. Sometimes we feel strong in the face of it, sometimes unable to cope. Somehow, eventually, the crushing sense of sorrow and the pointlessness of life finds a way of moulding itself around the framework of everyday existence. It resides softly, sometimes re-emerging violently in unexpected times and places, but the initial paralysis it causes is no longer what it was and the possibility of life continuing can be contemplated.

Svalbard Journey

First Visit, 17 January 2013

As I walk in the newly emerging twilight of the early afternoon, I enjoy the glimpses of the surroundings which are revealed to me. I can see some of the details of the mountains, craggy glacial folds and ridges beneath the snow, and a long, sharp, flat summit running along the very top of the skyline, the crest of which seems to have been highlighted with a white marker pen. I see the disused paraphernalia of the coal mining industry, long obsolete, except for a small local concern which serves Longyearbyen alone. I notice paths I have not seen before, and that a man who passes me by is not wearing gloves (which in this biting, wind-driven cold is most notable). And I am grateful to be able to see these finer points—even if only in shadow—as the frustration of the dark season has begun to impinge upon me and I find myself longing to see the fullness of the beauty of this mysterious and remote place. Then, just as suddenly as it appears at this time of January, the distant southern light disappears, plunging the vista into semi-blackness once again. I look up, and realize that during that hour or so of eye-opening light, I have not been able to see the stars. Gradually they rematerialize into my vision, almost one by one, the Northern Pole star hanging directly above my head, holding the axis of the earth firmly in its grasp. It is an obvious thing, of course, but even the dimmest and lowest of lights extinguishes the glow of the stars. And I am grateful once again for the rich profundity of the darkness and for the precious splendour which it alone can reveal.

VI

So maybe I do prefer the dark to the light, the night to the day; all I ask is that you do not judge me for it, certainly do not demonize me. Darkness is as wonderful and abundant with life as light. Darkness has its own nature and its own potency. And darkness is as much of God's making, as much of God's choice, as necessary for life, as the glorious and heavenly light.

A Poem to celebrate the Return of the Sun

Written on leaving Svalbard, March 2014

Farewell delectable darkness–
go gently,
held in the heart of God,
until we meet again.
And when You return
I shall run to embrace You.
For I shall miss your shadows and your deep blue night.
You make me still
and open my eyes to a different world beyond the obvious.
Your friend, the Light, will care for me well, I know.
But you are the source of life and until I see your face again,
reflected in the stars,
I shall not peacefully sleep.

Appendix: The Liturgical Darkness

Material for Reflection and Worship

A Prayer for the Morning

As a new day dawns and life goes on,
we give thanks for all that leads us into a sense of God's purpose and love;

We thank God for light
and for the presence of God it reveals among us.

We thank God for darkness
and for the promise of rest it represents to us.

We thank God for gathering
and for the grace-full challenge of connection with others.

A Prayer for the Evening

As evening approaches and life goes on,
we give thanks for all that leads us into a sense of God's purpose and love;

We thank God for darkness
and for the memories and longings it stirs within us.

We thank God for light
and for the hope and challenge it lays before us.

We thank God for gathering
and for the fine embrace of the closeness of others.

A Eucharistic Prayer

to share in the twilight

The Preparation

Dim the lights for Christ, our guest, is already here.
Close the blinds,
draw the curtains.
Light the candles,
plump the cushions.
Turn on the music.
All is prepared.
Welcome him into our home.
The table is set,
the food is ready.
Come, sit.
Let us talk of love and heavenly things.

Prayer of Thanksgiving

The Lord be with you
and also with you.

Lift up your hearts.
We lift them up to God.

Let us give thanks to the Lord our God.
It is right to give our thanks and praise.

Creator God, you were before all things; in darkness you dwelt, awaiting
the moment of universal formation; then, from the seed of your passion,
the dark gave birth to light and history began.

In time, and under the cover of night, Jesus was born, a gift of shade within a world that had become disorientated by brightness. We thank you that in him has been revealed your way of balance in which:
activity embraces stillness and speech embraces silence;
certainty embraces doubt and reason embraces intuition;
knowing embraces unknowing and light embraces darkness.

And so with angels and archangels and all the choirs of Heaven we join in the unending hymn of praise:
Holy, Holy, Holy Lord,
God of light and dark,
Heaven and earth reflect this glory.
Hosanna in the highest.
Blessed is One who comes in the name of the Lord.
Hosanna in the highest.

And as we give thanks, we recall how one evening, in a dimly lit upper room, Jesus took a loaf of bread, and after blessing it he broke it, gave it to them, and said, "Take; this is my body." Then he took a cup, and after giving thanks he gave it to them, and all of them drank from it. He said to them, "This is my blood of the covenant, which is poured out for many. Truly I tell you, I will never again drink of the fruit of the vine until that day when I drink it new in the kingdom of God."

Since that time the followers of Christ have met him in the sharing of bread and wine. It is a sublime sharing to which we come just as God made us. Around the table of the Lord we proclaim in praise and thanksgiving that we are wonderfully and fearfully made, and we celebrate that which is a mystery to us:
In darkness Christ died.
In darkness Christ rose.
In darkness Christ will come again.

Come now, tenebrous spirit, mysterious, comforting shadow. Transform these humble gifts of our table, bread and wine, into the living body and blood of Jesus Christ. As we share them, may we know the safety of God's darkness, offering us rest, renewal, and challenge.

The bread is broken and the bread and wine are shared.

Prayer Following the Meal

God of Balance, you have fed us with this heavenly food.
Bread which began as a grain of wheat buried in the soil.
Wine which began as a grape on the vine, with roots submerged deep.
In this celebration of life we have travelled into the darkness of the earth
and been lifted high into the glory of Heaven.
We have found a protective shade in the grace of Christ
and shelter in the companionship of others.
For these precious gifts which we have shared this night, we give you thanks.
Amen.

Blessing

May the Blessing of God
Who is
Darkness,
Love,
and Light
enfold us each day and each night
now and always.
Amen.

Hymn

Tune: From Sinking Sand He Lifted Me

The universe in darkness lay
when from the night God brought forth day
and so creation forged its way
in balanced harmony.

When night time falls, God shelters me.
When sorrow calls, God comforts me.
In darkest light, God holds me tight;
no need to fear, for God is here.

In darkness God reveals a face
which guides and leads us to a place
where freedom calls through time and space
for all humanity.

When Christ was born in deepest night
a star held vigil to the sight.
A gift of shade in blinding light
to pave the way for peace.

But still the world in brightness lay,
the star obscured by light of day.
And only in the darkest grave
could love break fin'lly free.

Upon the mount, or deep below
the earth, in darkness, I can know
that God is still creating, so
that life can go its way.

Hymn

Tune: Picardy

Looking out we seek the eternal,
searching in the dark for a light,
hoping for a sign of the Presence,
longing for the source of delight.
Reason takes its course but cannot reach the goal;
myst'ry shields the fountain of life.

Dare to name the language of absence,
dwell in the unknowing of God.
Live by faith but hold understanding,
follow where the saintly have trod.
Clarity comes faintly, words belie a truth.
Wisdom born in glimpses of night.

Twilight is the space of our dreaming,
even-tide when mourning shall cease.
Darkness is the place of renewal,
deep within, the birthing of peace.
Through the Shadows God speaks silently,
whispering the language of love.

A Meditation in the Dark

> I will give you the treasures of darkness
> and riches hidden in secret places,
> so that you may know that it is I, the Lord,
> who call you by your name.
>
> *Isaiah 45:3*

In darkness we seek the Lord,
unseen and unknown.
We claw at thin air and cry into the silence;
we read between the lines and clutch at straws.
All for a fragment of grace revealed in a shadow.

In darkness we seek the Lord.
Like many have before us.
Pilgrims and disciples who come to Jesus by night,
seeking answers, searching for truth, longing for healing.

In darkness God calls us.
Calls us to grow.
Calls us to feed.
Calls us to pray.
Calls us to love.
Calls us to work.
Calls us to rest.

For in darkness is the source of resurrection found.
Do not fear it.
Do not dread it.
Place yourself into God's heart;
absorb the beauty of the twilight to be found there.
Feel its embrace,
for it is a divine, sublime embrace.
And although God is light,
in him total darkness is found.

Treasure the Darkness

Trea-sure the   dark-ness, trea-sure the   shade,

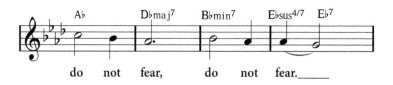

do   not   fear,   do   not   fear.____

Trea-sure the   dark-ness, watch the light fade,   do not

fear,   do not fear, for the night is of God's keep-ing

Notes

1. Kathleen Jamie, from the chapter "Darkness and Light" in *Findings* (Sort Of Books, 2005), p. 3. Reprinted here by permission of Sort of Books.

2. John Hull, *In the Beginning There was Darkness: a Blind Person's Conversation with the Bible* (SCM Press, 2001), p. 3.

3. Barbara Brown Taylor, *Learning to Walk in the Dark* (HarperOne, 2014).

4. I am grateful to the Revd. Keith Davies who, in conversation on this matter, articulated the idea of a "spirituality of balance".

5. William Horwood, *Skallagrigg* (Penguin Books, 1988), p. 81.

6. Rowan Williams, *The Poems of Rowan Williams* (Carcanet Press, 2014), p. 15.

7. <http://www.spainthenandnow.com/spanish-history/cordoba-historical-overview/default_41.aspx>.

8. Donald K. Carter and Stephen Quick with Remaking Cities Institute, *LED Street Light Research Project* (Pittsburgh, 2011).

9. Craig Koslofsky, *Evening's Empire: A History of the Night in Early Modern Europe* (Cambridge University Press, 2011).

10. <http://www.darkskydiscovery.org.uk/int_dark_sky_places.html>.

11. <https://www.mydarksky.com/home.aspx>.

12. <https://www.mydarksky.com/home.aspx>.

13. Used with permission.

14. T. S. Eliot, from "East Coker", *Four Quartets* (Faber Poetry, 2001).

15. Daniel O'Leary, "Caught Between Heaven and Earth", *The Tablet: The International Catholic News Weekly*, 15 April 2006. Reproduced with permission of the publisher. <http://www.thetablet.co.uk>.

16. Karl Rahner, tr. William V. Dych, *Foundations of Christian Faith: An Introduction to the Idea of Christianity* (Crossroad, 1989), p. 22.

17. Sharynne MacLeod NicMhacha, *Queen of the Night: Rediscovering the Celtic Moon Goddess* (Weiser Books, 2005), p. 138.

18. MacLeod NicMhacha, *Queen of the Night*, p. 142.

19. MacLeod NicMhacha, *Queen of the Night*, p. 138.

20. The Biblical Illustrator, Electronic Database. Copyright © 2002, 2003, 2006, 2011 by Biblesoft, Inc. <http://biblehub.com/sermons/auth/pulsforal/the_changes_of_the_sky.htm>

21. John Milton, *Paradise Lost*, from Book 1. Emphasis added.

22. Henry Vaughan, "The Night".

23. Brian Wren, *Joyful is the Dark* (Stainer and Bell, 1989).

24. Denys the Areopagite, "The Mystical Theology", in Pseudo-Dionysius, tr. Colm Luibheid, *The Complete Works*, Classics of Western Spirituality 54 (Paulist Press, 1987), p. 135.

25. Denys Turner, *The Darkness of God: Negativity in Christian Mysticism* (Cambridge University Press, 1995).

26. Turner, *The Darkness of God*, pp. 17–18.

27. Denys the Areopagite, "The Mystical Theology", p. 139.

28. Chris Fitter, "The Poetic Nocturne: From Ancient Motif to Renaissance Genre", in *Early Modern Literary Studies* 3.2 (1997), 2.1–61; <http://purl.oclc.org/emls/03-2/fittnoct.html>.

29. Craig Koslofsky, *Evening's Empire: A History of the Night in Early Modern Europe* (Cambridge University Press, 2011), p. 13.

30. Richard Rohr in an interview with Jonathan Langley to be found at <https://issuu.com/bmsworldmission/docs/mission_catalyst_mystery>. Emphasis in the original.

31. <http://www.torch.ox.ac.uk/wittenberg-nightingale-trigger-hans-sachs%E2%80%99-success-voice-reformation-nuremberg>.

32. Maximilianus Sandaeus, *Pro theologia mystica clavis: elucidarium onomasticon vocabulorum et loquutionum obscurarum* (Éditions de la Bibiotheque S.J., 1963; facsimile of Cologne: Officina Gualteriana, 1640).

33. John Donne, as found in *The Methodist Worship Book* (Methodist Publishing House, 1999), p. 459.

34. John of the Cross, tr. E. Allison Peers, "Dark Night of the Soul", in *The Essential St John of the Cross* (Wilder Publications, 2008), p. 475.

35. John of the Cross, "Dark Night of the Soul", p. 646.

36. George Herbert, ed. John Tobin, *The Complete English Poems* (Penguin, 1991), p. 191. Copyright © John Tobin, 1991, 2004.

37. Antony Horneck, quoted in Koslofsky, *Evening's Empire*, p. 2.

38. Koslofsky, *Evening's Empire*, p. 66.

39. Koslofsky, *Evening's Empire*.

40. Jack Finegan, *An Archaeological History of Religions of Indian Asia* (Paragon House, 1989), p. 37.

41. Anat Geva and Anuradha Mukherji, "The Holy Darkness: A Study of Light in Brihadeshvara Hindu Temple, Tanjore, Tamil Nadu, India (1010 AD)"; <http://papers.cumincad.org/data/works/att/sigradi2006_e185d.content.pdf>.

42. <http://www.srilankaguardian.org/2011/08/in-veneration-of-nallurs-virama-kali.html>.

43. Lex Hixon, *Great Swan: Meetings with Ramakrishna* (Shambala Publications Inc, first edition, 1992), pp. 183–184.

44. *Qu'ran*, using the translation at <https://www.free-minds.org/quran/>.

45. René Guénon, tr. Henry D. Fohr, *The Great Triad* (Sophia Perennis et Universalis; second edition, 2002), pp. 26, 103.

46. Edmund Burke, ed. Adam Phillips, *A Philosophical Enquiry into the Origin of Our Ideas of the Sublime and Beautiful* (Oxford University Press, 1998), p. 36.

47. Burke, *A Philosophical Enquiry,* p. 54.

48. John Locke, *An Essay Concerning Human Understanding* (Bibliolife, 2009), p. 72.

49. Burke, *A Philosophical Enquiry*, p. 130.

50. American Academy of Sleep Medicine, "Some adults with sleep disturbances are actually afraid of the dark, study says", *Science Daily*, 11 June 2012, <http://www.sciencedaily.com/releases/2012/06/120611092343.htm>.

51. Disabled World e-newsletter (October 2010), <http://www.disabled-world.com/health/neurology/phobias/nyctophobia.php#ixzz2KnS6DHDX>.

52. Directed by Roland Emmerich, 2009.

53. Flagship Studios, 2007.

54. Posted by Michelangelo on 9 March 2012 on <http://www.johncoulthart.com>.

55. Tom Phillips, "To Wander the Void" in *Vast Oceans Lachrymose* (2012).

56. James Attlee, *Nocturne: A Journey in Search of Moonlight* (Penguin Books, 2011).

57. Attlee, *Nocturne*, p. 39.

58. Attlee, *Nocturne*, p. 40.

59. Heather Ward, Nigel Shepherd, Sandy Robertson, and Mary Thomas, "Nighttime accidents: A scoping study"; Report to The AA Motoring Trust and Rees Jeffreys Road Fund (Centre for Transport Studies, University College London, October 2005).

60. <http://london.danslenoir.com>.

61. John Buchan, *The Path of the King* (Create Space Independent Publishing Platform, 2016), p. 2.

62. Christiane Ritter, *A Woman in the Polar Night* (Greystone Books, 2010), p. 157.

63. Novalis, tr. George MacDonald, ed. Carol Appleby, *Hymns to the Night and Spiritual Songs* (Crescent Moon Publishing, 2010), "Hymn of the Night" III, p. 40.

64. New Revised Standard Version of the Bible.

65. New International Version of the Bible.

66. New Revised Standard Version of the Bible.

67. Mircea Eliade, *Myths, Dreams and Mysteries: The Encounter between Contemporary Faiths and Archaic Realities* (Harper & Row, 1967).

68. <https://www.historicenvironment.scot/visit-a-place/places/maeshowe-chambered-cairn-via-stenness>.

69. Martin Lowenthal, *Dawning of Clear Light: A Western Approach to Tibetan Dark Retreat Meditation* (Hampton Roads Publishing, 2003), p. 1.

70. Lowenthal, *Dawning of Clear Light*, pp. 3, 4.

71. A summary of her experiences can be seen at<https://www.youtube.com/watch?v=nhikzbGop20>. See also <http://darknessretreat.net/tag/darkness-retreats/>.

72. Josef Hargrave, Florence Lam, Chris Luebkeman, and Leni Schwendinger, *Cities Alive: Rethinking the Shades of Night* (Arup, <www.arup.com>, March 2015).

73. Jørgen Berge, "Mare Incognitum—Ecological Processes during the Polar Night" (A research project of UiT, The University of Norway Department of Arctic and Marine Biology, 2014).

74. For example, T. A. Bedrosian, R. J. Nelson, and Z. M. Weil, "Chronic dim light at night provokes reversible depression-like phenotype: possible role for TNF", in *Molecular Psychiatry* 18.8, pp. 930–936 (August 2013); published online July 2012, <https://www.researchgate.net/publication/229552757_Chronic_dim_light_at_night_provokes_reversible_depression-like_phenotype_Possible_role_for_TNF>.

75. Joshua J. Gooley, Kyle Chamberlain, Kurt A. Smith, Sat Bir S. Khalsa, Shantha M. W. Rajaratnam, Eliza Van Reen, Jamie M. Zeitzer, Charles A. Czeisler, and Steven W. Lockley, "Exposure to Room Light before Bedtime Suppresses Melatonin Onset and Shortens Melatonin Duration in Humans", in *The Journal of Clinical Endocrinology and Metabolism* 96.3 (March 2011), pp. 463–472; published online, November 2010.

76. Terry Pratchett, *Reaper Man* (Corgi, 1994), p. 263.

77. A translation offered in Lewis Spence, *The Popol Vuh: The Mythic and Heroic Sagas of the Kichés of Central America* (David Nutt, 1908), p. 217.

78. C. S. Lewis, *The Magician's Nephew* (Harper Collins Children's Books, 2001), p. 117.

79. It is from Shakespeare's *Macbeth*!

80. Da Vinci was familiar with the *"camera obscura"* which was the precursor of the modern camera.

81. Jenny Boyd with Holly George-Warren, *It's Not Only Rock 'n' Roll* (John Blake Publishing, 2013), p. 111.

82. Josef Hargrave, Florence Lam, Chris Luebkeman, and Leni Schwendinger, *Cities Alive: Rethinking the Shades of Night* (Arup, <www.arup.com>, March 2015), p. 61.

83. Hargrave, Lam, Luebkeman, and Schwendinger, *Cities Alive*, p. 30.

84. Junichiro Tanizaki, tr. Thomas J. Harper and Edward J. Seidensticker, *In Praise of Shadows* (Vintage Books, 2001). Reproduced by permission of The Random House Group Ltd. © 1991.

85. Tanizaki, *In Praise of Shadows*, p. 9.

86. Tanizaki, *In Praise of Shadows*, p. 32.

87. Tanizaki, *In Praise of Shadows*, pp. 32–33.

88. Tanizaki, *In Praise of Shadows*, p. 20.

89. Tanizaki, *In Praise of Shadows*, p. 20.

90. Danny Schmidt, "Stained Glass", on *Parables and Primes* (2005).

91. <http://www.npr.org/2011/03/01/134160717/meditation-and-modern-art-meet-in-rothko-chapel>.

92. <http://www.npr.org/2011/03/01/134160717/meditation-and-modern-art-meet-in-rothko-chapel>.

93. N. Kawai, H. Miyata, R. Nishimura, and K. Okanoya, "Shadows Alter Facial Expressions of Noh Masks" (2013); PLoS ONE 8(8): e71389 <https://doi.org/10.1371/journal.pone.0071389>.

94. Alessandro Soranzo and Michelle Newberry, "The 'uncatchable smile' illusion in Da Vinci's Bella Principessa depends on the viewing angle", <http://www.sciencedirect.com/science/article/pii/S0042698915002163>.

95. <https://www.nationalgallery.org.uk/paintings/learn-about-art/paintings-in-depth/mysterious-virgin?viewPage=4>.

96. BBC 6Music, *John Grant's Songs from a Dark Place*, first transmitted on 24 December 2016 <http://www.bbc.co.uk/programmes/b04vk1gd>.

97. John Marriott, *Singing the Faith* (The Methodist Church/Hymns Ancient and Modern Ltd, 2011), No. 106, verses 1 and 3.

98. Charles Wesley, *Singing the Faith*, No. 134, from verse 1.

99. Extract from the song "Christmas is coming" by John L. Bell in *Inkeepers & Light Sleepers* (Wild Goose Publications, 1992). Copyright © WGRG, c/o Iona Community, Glasgow, Scotland. Reproduced by permission. <http://www.wildgoose.scot>

100. Extract from the song "Arise Shine" by Graham Kendrick in *Singing the Faith*, No. 170, verse 1. Copyright © 1985 Thankyou Music (adm. by CapitolCMGPublishing.com excl. UK & Europe, adm. by Integrity Music, part of the David C Cook family, songs@integritymusic.com).

101. Extract from the song "Indescribable" by Laura Story (additional lyrics Jesse Reeves) in *Singing the Faith*, No. 48, from verse 2. Copyright © 2004 worshiptogether.com Songs/sixsteps Music/Laura Stories (adm. by CapitolCMGPublishing.com excl. UK, adm. by Integrity Music, part of the David C Cook family, songs@integritymusic.com).

102. Extract from the song "In the darkness of the still of the night" by Margaret Rizza in *Singing the Faith*, No. 109, from verse 1. Copyright © Kevin Mayhew Ltd. Reproduced by permission of Kevin Mayhew Ltd <http://www.kevinmayhew.com>. Licence no. KMCL190517/01.

103. Extract from the song "I watch the sunrise" by John Glynn in *Singing the Faith*, No. 469, verses 3 and 4. Copyright © Kevin Mayhew Ltd. Reproduced by permission of Kevin Mayhew Ltd <http://www.kevinmayhew.com>. Licence no. KMCL190517/01.

104. Charles Wesley, *Singing the Faith*, No. 459, from verse 1.

105. Andrew Huth, in *BBC Proms: The Official Guide, 18 July–13 September 2014* (Ebury Press, 2014), p. 6.

106. Jalal al-Din Rumi, tr. Olwen Roy-Badziak, "The Song of the Night", in *BBC Proms: The Official Guide, 18 July–13 September 2014*, p. 10.

107. Novalis, tr. George Macdonald, ed. Carol Appleby, *Hymns to the Night and Spiritual Songs* (Crescent Moon Publishing, 2010), "Hymn of the Night" I, p. 37.

108. Attributed to Ban Ki-Moon.

109. Chimamanda Ngozi Adichie, "Lights Out in Nigeria", in *The New York Times Sunday Review*, 31 January 2015; <https://www.nytimes.com/2015/02/01/opinion/sunday/lights-out-in-nigeria.html>.

110. Matthew Beaumont, *Night walking: A Nocturnal History of London* (Verso, 2015), p. 5.

111. Beaumont, *Night walking*.

112. Bryan D. Palmer, *Cultures of Darkness: Night Travels in the Histories of Transgression* (Monthly Review Press, 2000), pp. 16–17.

113. Taken from an interview conducted as part of a night bus ride fundraising action by staff and friends of Hackney Migrant Centre in 2015, used with permission. Names have been changed.

114. Ben Okri, "To An English Friend in Africa", in *An African Elegy* (Jonathan Cape, 1992), p. 82.

115. I appropriate here the expression used by the Revd John Wesley when, in 1739, he experienced a life-changing spiritual conversion.

116. Brian Wren, *What Language Shall I Borrow? God-Talk in Worship: A Male Response to Feminist Theology* (SCM Press, 1989), p. 83.

117. Elisabeth Schüssler Fiorenza, *In Memory of Her: A Feminist Theological Reconstruction of Christian Origins* (SCM Press, 1983).

118. Dorothee Soelle, *The Strength of the Weak: Toward a Christian Feminist Identity* (Westminster Press, 1984).

119. Mark Haddon, *The Curious Incident of the Dog in the Night-time* (Vintage, 2004), pp. 19–20.

120. Taken from Luke Timothy Johnson, *The Creed: What Christians Believe and Why It Matters* (DLT, 2003), p. 5. Copyright 2003 by Darton Longman and Todd Ltd, London, and used by permission of the publishers.

121. See, for example, Paul Alan Laughlin, "A Mystical Christian Credo", in Charles W. Hedrick (ed.), *When Faith meets Reason: Religion Scholars Reflect on their Spiritual Journeys* (Polebridge Press, 2008) and "The World Methodist Social Affirmation" (World Methodist Council, 1986); <http://worldmethodistcouncil. org/wp-content/uploads/2012/04/WMC-Social-Affirmation.pdf>.

122. Definition of "metaphor" from *Shorter Oxford English Dictionary 6E* (Oxford University Press, 2007) by permission of Oxford University Press.

123. Wren, *What Language Shall I Borrow?*, p. 107.

124. Wren, *What Language Shall I Borrow?*, p. 68.

125. Wren, *What Language Shall I Borrow?*, p. 108.

126. John Milton, *Paradise Lost* (Penguin Books, 2003), pp. 227–228.

127. John Donne, *The Collected Poems of John Donne* (Wordsworth Editions Ltd, 1994), p. 50.

Lightning Source UK Ltd.
Milton Keynes UK
UKHW02f1013201117
313027UK00012B/795/P